The Complete Guide to Investing in

REITs

Real Estate Investment Trusts

How to Earn High Rates of Return Safety

By Mark Gordon

THE COMPLETE GUIDE TO INVESTING IN REITS — REAL ESTATE INVESTMENT TRUSTS: HOW TO EARN HIGH RATES OF RETURN SAFETY

1405 SW 6th Ave. • Ocala, Florida 34471 • 800-814-1132 • 352-622-1875–Fax
Web site: www.atlantic-pub.com • E-mail: sales@atlantic-pub.com
SAN Number: 268-1250

ISBN-13: 978-1-60138-256-6   ISBN-10: 1-60138-256-1

Library of Congress Cataloging-in-Publication Data

Gordon, Mark, 1974-
The complete guide to investing in REITs — real estate investment trusts: how to earn high rates of return safely / by Mark Gordon.
   p. cm.
Includes bibliographical references and index.
ISBN-13: 978-1-60138-256-6 (alk. paper)
ISBN-10: 1-60138-256-1 (alk. paper)
1. Real estate investment trusts--United States. 2. Real estate investment trusts--United States--Case studies. I. Title.

HG5095.G56 2008
332.63'2470973--dc22
                2008025886

Printed on Recycled Paper

INTERIOR LAYOUT DESIGN: Nicole Deck ndeck@atlantic-pub.com

Printed in the United States

THE HUMANE SOCIETY
OF THE UNITED STATES ©

The human-animal bond is as old as human history. We cherish our animal companions for their unconditional affection and acceptance. We feel a thrill when we glimpse wild creatures in their natural habitat or in our own backyard.

Unfortunately, the human-animal bond has at times been weakened. Humans have exploited some animal species to the point of extinction.

The Humane Society of the United States makes a difference in the lives of animals here at home and worldwide. The HSUS is dedicated to creating a world where our relationship with animals is guided by compassion. We seek a truly humane society in which animals are respected for their intrinsic value and where the human-animal bond is strong.

Want to help animals? We have plenty of suggestions. Adopt a pet from a local shelter, or join The Humane Society and be a part of our work to help companion animals and wildlife. You will be funding our educational, legislative, investigative and outreach projects in the United States and across the globe.

Or perhaps you'd like to make a memorial donation in honor of a pet, friend or relative? You can through our Kindred Spirits program. If you'd like to contribute in a more structured way, our Planned Giving Office has suggestions about estate planning, annuities and even gifts of stock that avoid capital gains taxes.

Maybe you have land that you would like to preserve as a lasting habitat for wildlife. Our Wildlife Land Trust can help you. Perhaps the land you want to share is a backyard — that's enough. Our Urban Wildlife Sanctuary Program will show you how to create a habitat for your wild neighbors.

So you see, it's easy to help animals, and The HSUS is here to help.

The Humane Society of the United States
2100 L Street NW
Washington, DC 20037
202-452-1100
www.hsus.org

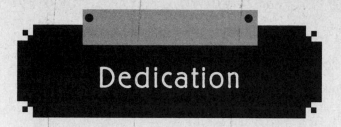

Dedication

This book is dedicated to Elyse, the most supportive wife in the world. If she were an investment, her symbol would be BWE. And to Uncle Junior, whose trusted shtick (almost) never gets old.

Table of Contents

Introduction

In some ways, a book with "real estate" and "trust" in the title could be a tough sell. The real estate industry has not built up much trust with the public over the last two years or so, as, nationwide, the once-sizzling real estate market has cooled significantly.

Nonetheless, real estate, in one form or another, remains one constant in everyone's life. Real estate is everywhere, from the home or office where this book is being read to the home it was written in to the printing press to where it was published. Essentially, the portfolio of real estate lasts an entire life, from the hospital wing where babies are born to the nursing home room, where some people spend their last days.

The barren ground in a given area is real estate. Maybe it is a plot of land owned by a county or municipal government, where officials plan on building a school. Maybe it is a massive swath of land where a national homebuilder plans on developing thousands of homes. (There has not been much of the latter the past two years, as developers and big-ticket land buyers wait out the market.)

The golf course with the tough ninth hole, the park where the children play in the sandbox, the local mall, and the town hall all fall under the real-estate banner. Many iconic landmarks are, at their core, real estate too, such as the Empire State Building, the Sears Tower, and even the famed Seattle fish market.

Still, beyond using real estate for its given function, the industry, especially the commercial real estate side of it, remains mysterious to many. To be sure, millions of people buy and sell houses every year, even in a slumping market, and millions more rent a home or an apartment.

Outside those purchases, though, few people realize who individually owns all this real estate and how a certain building was even built in the first place. A name like Donald Trump might make newspaper headlines for splashy ownership of a few luxury condo buildings, but, as big as the Trump name is, his holdings are miniscule when compared to the real-estate portfolio that exists in the entire country.

Turns out a more substantial chunk of commercial real estate holdings, collectively, are owned by millions of people significantly less rich and significantly more anonymous than Trump. They might own a tiny piece of a strip mall, a small part of a warehouse, or maybe a share of a mortgage portfolio.

This kind of ownership is accomplished through investing in a real estate investment trust, better known as a REIT (rhymes with beet).

This book attempts to explain the ins, outs, ups, and downs of REITs as well as the history of the investment and how it all relates to an investor's biggest predictor of future success: risks and rewards.

There are more than 200 publicly traded REITs in the United States, with assets totaling more than $450 billion. REITs, at least the ones that are real-estate holding companies, can control a wide variety of assets, everything from apartment complexes to zoos. Those REITs are known as equity REITs.

Other REITs, dubbed mortgage REITs, are essentially holding companies for mortgage portfolios. A third type of real estate investment trust, which combines the other two styles, is called a hybrid REIT.

With that as a backdrop, a good place to start a REIT tutorial is explaining the characteristics of a REIT, or better yet, what makes a REIT so special that it warrants its own book anyway?

The first section of this book, *A Meet and REIT*, focuses on that question, with five chapters detailing the life and times of a REIT. Created in 1960 by the U.S. Congress, the original purpose of a REIT was to "allow people from all walks of life to invest in a diversified, professionally managed real estate enterprise," according to a 1999 congressional presentation given by Tony M. Edwards, then the senior vice president and general counsel of the National Association of Real Estate Investment Trusts, the industry's leading trade and lobbying group.

In many ways, the plan has been successful. REITs are now sought after by countless conservative-thinking, long-term investors, individuals and institutions both. REITs, by definition, must return at least 90 percent of their annual taxable income to shareholders through dividends. In return for that commitment, Congress waived the corporate-level income tax on the investments, as long as they complied with other tax laws.

As is explained in more detail in Chapter 3, REITs were more than just a way for the average investor to play real estate mogul. REITs are not just a Monopoly game for the minions.

Indeed, in addition to providing low levels of risk with high levels of predictability, REITs have some investment-specific features, such as cash available for distribution (CAD). Sometimes referred to as funds available for distribution (FAD), this is a REIT's ability to dispense cash in the form of dividends to shareholders. In most case, this dividend is what is left over after a REIT accounts for both real estate and non-real estate related expenses.

Topics such as CADs and other technical aspects of REIT investing are explained in Chapter 3.

The second section of this book is a primer on all the types of real estate equity REITs available on the market. An equity REIT is set up to buy and develop properties for ownership and rental purposes; it does not strictly build and sell properties like a developer might do.

Equity REITs are like extended families. They can be made up of many parts, sometimes spread out nationwide that individually have different roles but collectively form one unit. In practice, that adds up to a variety of REIT sectors.

The families that make up a REIT fall under the following categories: residential, office, retail, industrial, healthcare, hotels, self-storage facilities, and manufactured homes. Those REIT categories are explained in more detail in the second section of the book, Chapters 6 through 13.

The third section of this book deals with the concept of buying and selling shares of REITs. There are a significant amount of options — more than 200 equity REITs in almost a dozen categories.

As in any type of investing activity, choices sometimes breed risk. In the world of REITs, one potential risk is simple supply and demand, otherwise known as overbuilding and oversupply. That is, overbuilding of a certain property type in a certain market can lead to falling rental rates, as the availability of the property outpaces the demand.

Declining rents, in turn, can lead to an decline in the resale value of the property.

Another risk factor that can negatively affect REITs in similar, domino-like fashion is rising interest rates. To start with, higher interest rates mean higher borrowing costs, which tend to shrink a REIT's long-term return.

Higher interest rates also tend to hit the entire economy hard, which in turn can lead to less need for real-estate properties, bringing the supply-and-demand issue back into the picture.

Additionally, rising interest rates are sometimes followed by declining stock prices in REITs, as well as the entire stock market. For REITs though, an interest rate pushback on share prices can have a long-term effect, as investors seek higher yields elsewhere, such as in bonds.

There are more REIT-specific risks, too. Many of those are detailed in Chapter 16.

And the future of the REIT industry — still a youngster in investment years, having been born in 1960 — shows major promise, especially given technology advancements that are providing more access to research, information, and data than ever before.

Even this decade, the industry has achieved some major milestones.

In 2001, for example, after several years of industry lobbying, a REIT finally gained inclusion to the family of Standard & Poor's U.S. indices when Chicago-based Equity Office Properties replaced Texaco on the S&P 500. (Equity Office Properties has since been bought by a private equity firm and no longer is a publicly traded entity).

Following Equity Office Properties, other REITs were placed in indices such as the S&P 400 MidCap index and the S&P SmallCap 600 index. In late 2007, there were 13 REITs on the S&P 500, 15 REITs on the S&P 400 MidCap index, and 18 REITs on the S&P SmallCap 600 index.

Inclusion on these indices, such as the well-followed S&P 500, is considered to be an invitation to a bigger investment platform. Indeed, in placing REITs on the indices for the first time, Standard & Poor's advanced the REIT cause even further by stating it believes, "REITs have become operating companies subject to the same economic and financial factors as other publicly traded companies listed on major American stock exchanges."

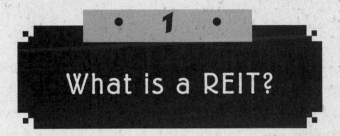

· 1 ·
What is a REIT?

Ever since the first stock traders gathered outside the then brand-new New York Stock Exchange in 1792, someone somewhere has been searching for the perfect, high-return, risk-free investment.

The search, obviously, has been futile. All types of investments carry risk. Even not investing in a certain option carries its own risk.

Nonetheless, in 1960 the U.S. Congress created an investment vehicle where the goal, at least initially, was to give investors a chance to own a stake in real estate while simultaneously owning a stake in a traditional trust. It was an attempt, in some regards, at creating a near-perfect investment tool by combining the risk of real-estate ownership with the tidiness of trusts. It also allowed individual real-estate investors the opportunity to pool their money together for the same benefits as traditional real-estate owners.

Simply, albeit with little flair in its name, this government-created tool was called a real estate investment trust.

As this was a government operation, there were some basic stipulations put into place right from the beginning. These rules turned out to be wise.

First, Congress waived the corporate-level income tax on REITs, as long as they complied with other tax laws. This was especially important because before the law, a standard property-owning company would be paying taxes twice, in a corporate tax and a dividend tax. Now a REIT investor would be paying taxes only on dividends, at a personal income tax rate. And fewer taxes, in turn, would mean more money going to investors for either personal gain, or, in many cases, reinvestment in the REIT.

Federal legislators then determined that would make up a REIT. In turn, the company must place at least 75 percent of its investments in real estate, while at the same time, 75 percent of its income most be derived from mortgage interest or rental income.

Another REIT rule states that no more than 30 percent of the trust's annual income can come from the sale of properties held fewer than four years. That is so a REIT does not use its special tax status while morphing into a developer or other real estate company that regularly buys and sells properties.

Because part of the intention in REITs was to make them accessible for all investors, even those with limited finances, Congress instituted a 100/50 rule: A REIT's shares must be owned by at least 100 people, and no more than 50 percent of the trust can be owned by five or fewer individuals during the last half of each taxable year.

In addition, there is this: lawmakers stipulated that to be a

REIT, the company must return at least 90 percent of its annual taxable income to shareholders through dividends. That particular caveat has been one of the REIT's most enduringly popular features.

After absorbing those roles, a publicly traded REIT shares many attributes of a publicly traded company. It has a board of directors; a standard company hierarchy chart, from chairman and chief executive officer on down; it is traded on one of several stock exchanges; and it issues stock, in common, convertible, and preferred forms.

The big difference between a REIT and shares of a straight-up public company is in the yield, which is when investors receive a percentage of the market price of the investment trust's shares. The yield is calculated by dividing the dividend into the share price; so, for example, if a REIT is trading at $100 a share and provides a dividend of $8.25, then the yield is 8.25 percent.

Similar to the bond market, if the shares move up but the dividend remains the same, then the yield will fall. In the bond market though, bonds tend to rise, and their yields tend to fall when investors are seeking a way to mitigate their risk by getting money out of stocks.

REITs, on the other hand, tend to follow stock prices, not bonds, and in that way a REIT trades more like a stock. Also, REIT income, due to the fluctuating real-estate market, is not fixed income like a bond's income is. The added risk means a REIT will trade at least two percentage points higher than government or municipal bonds.

This all-important yield is essentially determined by REIT

managers. Good managers of REITs, just like executives of any other company, public or private, are constantly trying to cut costs, improve efficiencies, and increase profits. There are many ways a REIT executive can do that, from renovating a building to charge higher rents, to selling off underperforming assets.

The first three-plus decades of REITs were marked by boom-and-bust periods, as it swayed along with the entire U.S. economy. The 1962 stock market fall and subsequent mid-1960s rebound, the inflation and high gas prices period of the 1970s, the savings and loan crisis and government bailout of the 1980s, and the building parade of the 1990s all have played a role in the growth and development of the REIT. The life and times of the REIT has been more good than bad, as REIT operators tinkered with strategies, and investors attempted to figure out how to best use the investment vehicle.

The 1990s represented the most important, and by many financial readings, the biggest growth spurt yet for REITs. It came at a time, in the early part of the decade, when the country was going through a real estate downturn that turned into a housing recession in some areas.

Some in the financial and real estate industry cite that early 1990s housing recession as just the sort of catapult REITs needed to go mainstream: the real estate companies that survived the hard times, both big and small, needed access to capital — and fast. The answer, many of these companies realized, was to go public.

One of the first big private real-estate companies to go public was New York-based Kimco Realty. The company raised

$128 million in its 1991 IPO, a nice boost for shareholders and even nicer boost for the undiscovered REIT sector. After Kimco's IPO, according to industry trade group the National Association of Real Estate Investment Trusts (NAREIT), the floodgates opened for REITs. For example, the two-year period from 1993 to 1994 set an all-time REIT growth record, as almost 100 companies went public during that time, raising $16 billion in the process.

The next ten-plus years, continuing into 2008, represent something of a golden era for REITs. The product, essentially, has gone from being something on the back of a shelf that is constantly overlooked to one that is out in front and a legitimate option for all sorts of investors, both institutions and individuals. REITs have gone mainstream.

Indeed, from 1992 to 2004, the industry increased more than 20 times, from $16 billion to $308 billion. In 2001, REITs received a public endorsement when Standard & Poor's added a REIT investment class to its major indexes, including the S&P 500.

REITs, and REIT-owned property, can be found in just about any state, city, and town. Holdings under REITs include such landmark commercial real estate properties as the Mall of America in Bloomington, Minnesota, the Embarcadero Center in San Francisco, and the Merchandise Mart in Chicago. As of early 2008, according to NAREIT, there were about 200 publicly traded REITs in the United States, worth more than $450 billion in total assets.

In addition, in the United States, there are publicly registered REITs that do not trade over the exchanges or are otherwise privately held.

That is just a domestic count of publicly traded REITs. The investment tools also trade overseas, in at least 30 countries, including China, Mexico, and Poland.

REITs debuted in Hong Kong in 2005, for instance, and shares of the $2 billion-plus portfolio increased 15 percent on the first trading day. The Japanese REIT market has also grown significantly since investors started buying and trading the investment vehicles in 2001.

What is more, as recently as November 2007, real-estate and financial executives in countries without REITs were clamoring for them, too. For example, Anna Birulés, an executive with Spanish property group Renta Corporacion Real Estate SA — and the country's former science and technology minister — in a late 2007 speech publicly called on the Spanish government to introduce REITs.

Birulés, according to a report from Charlottesville, Virginia-based research and advisory firm SNL Financial, said REITs would help the country offset its real-estate market slowdown, and their tax benefits would generate more economic activity, including attracting more foreign investors.

A Trio of Options

In the United States there are three types of REITs, and in turn, those can be broken up into many smaller sub-categories. The big three are equity REITs, which own and operate income-producing real estate, from apartment buildings to self-storage centers; mortgage REITs, which lend money directly to real estate owners or buy loans and other mortgage-connected securities; and hybrid REITs, which are companies that own a variety of properties and make loans to other owners.

By definition, an equity REIT sounds a lot like a standard real estate company that buys, builds, and sells properties. The big difference between the two, though, is a REIT is set up only to buy and develop its properties for ownership, as opposed to simply building and selling off properties.

Equity REITs can be made up of many different parts — if it comes out of the ground, has four walls and a roof, and can be bought and sold, then in some way it potentially could be part of an equity REIT. That includes hotels and hospitals, shopping malls and warehouses, condos, and apartments. Equity REITs can also be geographically wrapped, such as covering the Southeast United States or only the West Coast. Specifics on REIT sectors are detailed later in the book.

Equity REITs present investors with different, sometimes dueling investing strategies. Some equity REITs, such as ones that seek what is known as a triple net lease, have slow and low growth potential, while steadily producing high dividends. Other equity REITs, such as ones that develop new property, produce lower dividend returns but have higher growth potential.

Meanwhile, most mortgage REITs will sell mortgages only for existing properties, managing risk through mortgage securities and hedging processes. Currently, mortgage REITs are only involved in loaning money to existing properties, whereas in the past the operators of the trust also made construction and development loans.

Investors buying a mortgage REIT tend to be seeking

high-dividend returns, as by nature mortgage REITs are not built to provide high appreciation results — there is no real property to appreciate. Indeed, mortgage REITs will see a significant value bump only if interest rates steadily decline. It also holds that if interest rates go up, the value of the REIT will likely go down.

Today's mortgage REIT portfolio is big on diversification, combining a variety of mortgage pools to form one REIT. Those pools come from a variety of sources, from government lending agencies to large Wall Street investment banks.

For the latter part of 2007 and into 2008, some mortgage REITs were making news for undesirable reasons, at least to their operators and shareholders. This was because of the nationwide residential real estate slowdown and the credit problems in the subprime lending industry that followed.

Those problems, for instance, engulfed NovaStar Financial Inc., a Kansas City-based subprime home lender and mortgage REIT in 2007. The company, with hundreds of underperforming loans in the hundreds of millions of dollars, informed shareholders September 17, 2007, that it would not be paying out a dividend on its 2006 profit, and instead it would be conserving cash as it went into survival mode. As a result, the company forfeited its REIT designation.

In a statement, the company put the onus of giving up REIT status on the troubled subprime market.

"Clearly, we did not anticipate the drop in market value or the level of demands on liquidity caused by the market turmoil this summer," said Scott Hartman, NovaStar's Chairman and

Chief Executive Officer, in the company statement. "Canceling the previously planned dividend is the only reasonable and prudent course of action."

What is more, losing REIT status hurt the company, and its shareholders, in more ways than just not having a dividend. Shares of the company dropped more than 100 percent through September 2007, and the company's New York Stock Exchange membership was jeopardized.

Mortgage REIT horror stories such as NovaStar are not, or at least have not been, commonplace.

Hybrid REITs are attempts at combining both attributes of equity and mortgage REITs. The healthcare sector is a popular destination for hybrid REITs, where the trust can provide mortgages to healthcare companies and hospital operators and buy properties, such as medical office parks, that lease space to healthcare companies.

Hybrids, not surprisingly, tend to provide a mix of potential results for investors; only the value of that mix is often questioned by the investing community. The dividend yields provided by hybrid REITs tend to be higher than equity REITs but lower than mortgage REITs. Also, hybrid REITs tend to have less growth appreciation than equity REITs but more growth appreciation than mortgage REITs.

One problem some investors have with hybrid REITs is that it might be too much diversification. That is, the strategies that drive mortgage and equity REITs are inherently different, so a REIT that combines both runs the risk of diluting the benefits while doubling the risks.

So which, out of the three REIT categories, is the best option?

For starters, some of that depends on what a particular investor is seeking — high growth rates in share prices, regular high dividends, or something in the middle.

In the 1970s, according to NAREIT, mortgage REITs were by far the life of the REIT party, holding about a three-to-one edge in investor allocations over equity REITs. In 1970, the count was almost 80 percent in mortgage REITs and 20 percent in equity REITs.

But over the next 30 years, those ratios would change, especially as the United States went through several sustained commercial and residential housing booms. By the mid 1980s, it was more of a 50-50 comparison, and through most of the 1990s and the current decade the three-to-one ratio was essentially reversed in favor of equity REITs.

Investor popularity aside, equity REITs have produced the best returns going back to the 1970s, NAREIT reports, while mortgage REITs have produced the highest dividend yield. Therefore, the consensus in the investing community today is that equity REITs are better bets for conservative investments, especially considering the current unpredictable status of the mortgage industry.

Leveraging Predictability

REITs have several features that separate the investment from what sometimes seems to be an endless list of investing possibilities. Individually, these features are nothing to brag about, but combined, the list provides real fodder for celebrating. Those features include:

Diversification: Because REITs are legally required to pay out 90 cents of every taxable income-generated dollar to shareholders, investors can steadfastly rely on the investment. Traditionally, this return competes with, and in some cases even outperforms, stocks, mutual funds, and bonds. NAREIT, for example, says a REIT dividend is, on average, four times higher than those of other stocks.

Low correlation: This, a second cousin of diversification, is a sometimes unappreciated, yet still important component of what makes REITs tick. Correlations, a standard measuring tool in the money managing and financial planning community, compare one asset class to another to predict what each class will do over time. So, for instance, analysts can see what affect a 5 percent rise in the S&P 500 Index has on stocks, or even REITs, by looking at the classes' historical correlations.

The correlation measurement ranges from a full -1, where the classes will do the complete opposite of each other, to a full +1, where the classes will be completely in sync with each other. The lower the correlation between two asset classes — say, stocks and bonds — the lower the volatility of the entire portfolio. That low correlation, in turn, increases the return rates of the entire portfolio.

REITs tend to have a low correlation, which means when the market is underperforming, or even in a bear-type atmosphere, REITs do little to drag an investment portfolio down even further. Of course, on the flip side, that low correlation tends to mean that when a certain index is rolling, such as say, the S&P 500, REITs bring little extra boost to the party.

In terms of raw numbers, NAREIT reports that the correlation of REIT returns with other investments has declined over the last 30 years. From 1994 to 2004, for example, the association reports REIT stocks had a .028 correlation when compared against the S&P 500 Index. Therefore, REIT fluctuations had only a 2.8 percent correlation with the S&P's telltale index.

Low risk/low volatility: Volatility is something most long-term investors shun, simply if only to limit their daily antacid intake. In turn, the less volatile a stock is, the less risky it tends to be.

No risk is a no-can-do possibility in investing. Every decision and non-decision involves some risk. Although equity REITs are a more sound investment than mortgage REITs, even those carry some risk that is out of investors' control. Those risks include the supply-and-demand forces at work in housing markets and ever-changing, complicated tax laws.

Specific REITs have risk too, mostly based on their given industry. Healthcare-based REITs have to contend with the problems of the healthcare industry, such as the decreasing rates of health insurance reimbursements, while retail REITs have to contend with the fickle attitudes of the American consumer.

Still, in the investment community, the inherent risk involved in REITs is widely seen as being significantly less than many other investments. A wide-ranging equity REIT could survive, even thrive, in a down market by diversifying its tenant list, its operating sector, and where its properties are located. For instance, a mall REIT can do well in a slumping retail market by changing out its roster of stores.

That is one way a REIT lowers the risk ratio as compared to a standard stock holding. Another way it does this is by simply not being a common stock holding.

That is, for reasons not completely understood by analysts — but likely having something to do with its diversity and predictability — REITs tend to not suffer from the Wall Street so-called surprise syndrome. That is when a company does well in a given quarter, even really well, but it does not "beat" the numbers Wall Street analysts had predicted. The company's shares then suffer, despite a good financial quarter.

Surprise syndrome is a growing situation on Wall Street, one that investors have been dealing with in some capacity since the boom in technology stocks of the late 1990s.

It has not made much of a difference in the REIT sector, though, further lowering the risk of investing in one.

Low leverage: The average REIT debt ratio has been below 50 percent the last 10 years or so, NAREIT reports. A low debt ratio, otherwise known as low leverage, can be a positive for several reasons, starting with the concept that the lower the leverage or debt, the lower the fixed costs a REIT (or a company) has. This might not help sales margins in some instances, but in the case of a REIT, it is another way of minimizing risk.

Predictability: In some regards, predictability goes back to why REITs were founded in 1960 in the first place. The mission was to create a stable investment tool for investors to rely on, to go with other more volatile and potentially less lucrative investment options.

Mission accomplished: From 1971 to 2006, equity REITs, as an asset class, had a compound annual return rate of 13.97 percent, according to NAREIT. That trumps the results produced by the Dow Jones Industrial Average (7.83 percent), the NASDAQ exchange (9.11 percent), and the S&P 500 Index (11.35 percent) over the same period.

Plus, REITs are not only predictable over the long term. They are also easy to gauge over the short term, due to the stable nature of the entity, such as rental and occupancy rates and expenses. Wall Street analysts normally come within a few cents every quarter of predicting financial results for individual REITs.

To be sure, predictability has its downside. Although there have been few front-page market mishaps involving REITs and the investment is a solid risk, a REIT is not likely to wow investors with gaudy returns. No one is likely to confuse even a high-performing REIT with shares of Google.

REITs have a small-to-medium equity market capitalization, according to NAREIT, and as such, their returns should be comparable to other small to mid-sized companies.

Liquidity: This is one of the more pleasant twists behind a REIT. For starters, a REIT controls individual real estate holdings, which are most decidedly not liquid. Real estate holdings can rarely, if ever, be sold easily, quickly, and at no discount — all of which need to be in play for an investment to be considered liquid. Yet a publicly traded stock is, in most cases, a liquid asset. Liquidity is a key component of making a quick and informed decision in investing and money management.

Value investments: Predictability, low volatility, and low correlation rates normally do not correspond with high-flying, even over-performing investments. But one possible explanation, according to some Wall Street analysts, is that REITs are a true value investment; that is, they are underpriced relative to their true value.

Big But Getting Bigger

Even factoring the boom of the 1990s and 2000s, REITs, many analysts say, still have a high upside, both as an entire asset class and as an investment option for individual investors. The $475-plus billion size of the industry, while big, is only a fragment of the $10 trillion-plus commercial real estate industry.

New laws and rules implemented between 1995 and 2005 give REIT supporters and investors even more reason for optimism. For example, a key piece of legislation that was passed in 1999 and went effect in 2001, the REIT Modernization Act, allows REITs to own what is known as a taxable REIT subsidiary. The bill, according to NAREIT, essentially provides an avenue for REIT holding companies to provide services to REIT tenants and others without disqualifying the rents that a REIT receives from its tenants.

But an even greater predictor of the future of REITs can be based simply on the past. The investments' steadily growing return ratios, even in a topsy-turvy market, just about ensure that the asset class will keep growing.

Real Estate Investments

S mart investing in the stock market is not as easy as simply calling a broker or logging onto the Internet and buying shares of IBM or Coca-Cola.

Stocks, right or wrong, sometimes carry baggage. For example, IBM's shares could suffer if another company in its sector has problems. Ditto for Coke: if another beverage company has a bad earnings report, then Coca-Cola's shares could drop with it. It is a common Wall Street occurrence.

Investors know this, and the savvy ones take that into account when deciding whether to buy the shares in the first place. Therefore, savvy investors tend to research not only the company holding the shares, but also the entire sector. Again using the Coca-Cola analogy, a buyer of Coke's shares should be well versed on the challenges, risks, and rewards of the entire beverage sector.

This theory holds true for real estate investing, too.

Right from the beginning, this concept presents more challenges than just being knowledgeable of the beverage industry. For one, that industry is easy to define: a company is either a beverage company or it is not — there is no gray area. Second, even in an Internet-driven research world, there is a limited, even manageable amount of sources to get information on the industry. That would be true for dozens of other sectors.

That is not so true for REITs.

The real estate industry is infinitely larger than most other industries. Indeed, as explained in the introduction, readers of this book have already taken part in several facets of the industry by simply holding this book: it was written in someone's house, edited in an office, printed in another location, and then stored and sold in yet another location. All of those structures are connected to real estate.

In a word, real estate is everywhere, as are real estate investment opportunities. The list ranges from strip malls to beachfront condos and from massive big-city apartment buildings to small-town manufactured-home communities.

Still, when researching the real estate industry to prepare for REIT investments, there are several successful formulas.

The most basic and proven concept in any real estate investment is the simple theory of supply and demand. Every real estate market is driven, to some extent, by the availability of property as compared to the market demand for the property in the given area.

In commercial real estate, factors such as population growth, job rates, and location weigh heavily on what the supply is and the demand is. Next, on a macro-basis, there are forces such as the state of the national economy, interest rates, and even gas prices.

Then, on a more micro-basis, there are other concerns, such as short-term and long-term expenses; quality, or lack thereof, of tenants in a given building; competition from other properties in the same market and segment; and cap rates, or the amount of cash flow an investor receives as a percentage of the purchase price.

These factors set the table nicely for a primer on the ups and downs of the real estate market.

The Spin Cycles

Real estate, if anything, is cyclical. In commercial real estate those cycles rotate on a different axis than residential real estate, the latter of which has its own, independent factors that drive the industry up and down.

In commercial real estate, one of those cycles of ups and downs is commonly known as a space market cycle, which involves the supply and demand for real estate space. A second cycle is called a capital market cycle, which is based on cash flow levels coming in and going out of real estate.

The space market cycle can be further broken down into four phases: depression, gradual recovery, boom and overbuilding, and downturn.

The first phase, depression, is marked by high vacancies and low rents. Tenants have the upper hand in negotiations and tend to win many concessions. Construction activity is minimal during this stage, while foreclosure activity, especially on buildings and projects financed with much debt, is high.

The next phase, a gradual recovery, is just that. During this period, slowly but surely, occupancy rates climb, rents go up, and the bargaining power between landlord and tenant is restored to something closer to 50-50. Development activity starts anew, too, during a gradual recovery, stopping just short of construction work.

The boom phase is when actual construction work becomes commonplace. The boom phase, while a positive development, is also sometimes known for excess, or in the now-famous words of former Federal Chairman Alan Greenspan, this phase could be considered "irrational exuberance." (Greenspan was referring to stock market fervor when he uttered those words on December 5, 1996, but it fits for real estate booms, too.)

Some of the other exuberant characteristics of a boom phase include rapidly increasing rents, as the top-tier space becomes occupied and supply wanes, as well as a financing floodgates, where lenders such as banks begin offering loans to all sorts of applicants, even ones they would have given second thoughts to during an early phase.

Finally, there is the overbuilding and downturn phase, an obvious follow-up to the boom. This is where the market becomes oversaturated with people — such as developers, speculators, and investors — who are all trying to capitalize on the good times. New buildings and available space turn the supply-and-demand factor more toward the consumer, which, in turn, brings down rental rates.

Then, the return on real estate investments begins to decline, and the investors begin to pull out their money and sell off their holdings. This downturn, depending on the severity, the market, and other factors, could then either revert to a recession, or, even worse, a depression.

But there is some good news among the space cycle reverberations.

For starters, space cycles, historically, have been getting longer in scope and less volatile, too, some economists and commercial real estate experts say, due to changes in the entire commercial real estate market landscape. The space market cycle of the late 1960s and 1970s lasted about 10 years, for example, and the next one lasted 21 years, from 1979 to 2000, according to U.S. congressional testimony from Glenn R. Mueller, a professor at the University of Denver's Franklin L. Burns School of Real Estate and Construction Management.

In Mueller's September 14, 2006, testimony, he said that even though the current commercial space market cycle "hit an occupancy bottom in 2003...price declines and loan defaults did not happen in this down cycle like they did in 1990."

Mueller, in his testimony before Congress's Subcommittee on Financial Institutions and Consumer Credit, added that the "space market cycle is still in recovery phase, with peak not expected until 2010."

After digesting the space market cycle of real estate, the next plate to consider is the capital markets cycle, which has been tougher to predict and project, as the source of that capital has gone from local to national to now international sources.

The capital cycle essentially refers to both the source and the amount of money coming into the commercial real estate sector. At its simplest, when capital flows in, real estate prices go up, which in turn could be positive for some REIT investors. Capital cycles tend to lag behind the space cycles, although occasionally the cycles are in rhythm with each other and property prices and property cash flows rise and fall in lockstep.

For investors thinking now is the time to consider REITs, the capital markets cycle is on a good part of the spin, according to some experts' analysis. For example, Mueller, in a section of his testimony regarding capital market cycles said, "the poor performance of the stock and bond markets since 2000 has pushed much more capital toward real estate in the United States because real estate is now seen as a safer and more stable investment."

Break It Down

But real estate investing and REITs must go deeper than simply examining the types and lengths of real estate cycles.

A good start is looking at the actual type of property. Some are more high-risk, with challenges, such as heavy management demands, short-term leases, and multiple competitors. Properties with a lower risk ratio tend to have a more predictable revenue stream and, as such, generate interest for individual investors.

The first dividing line is to figure out which properties are commercial real estate and which ones are not. A commercial real estate property is any building that is not a single-family home or multifamily home up to four units, a government-operated building, a farm or ranch, or raw land.

Going even further, some commercial properties are considered to be investment grade, which means the entities meet certain benchmarks and standards in size and quality to warrant interest from institutional investors.

In commercial real estate, a property's risk level is mostly determined by its capitalization rate. A cap rate is determined by dividing a property's post-expenses net operating income by its purchase price. The higher the cap rate, the higher the return will likely be, as well as the risk.

What follows is an examination of some of the various real estate sectors and the rewards, as well as the risks, each one holds for the real estate investing community.

Raw Land

This is, by far, the riskiest real estate investment; it has next to no tax benefits and no direct income stream. Also, because there is no revenue coming in, the costs — mortgage payments and taxes — are paid by the investor.

To be sure, the payoff comes by owning land in the right location, hence the "location, location, location" real estate axiom. If there turns out to be heavy demand, from say a shopping mall developer or a homebuilder, then land could be worth 10, 50, or even 100 times what an investor paid for it.

Raw land is a mixed bag for REITs because, despite the risks, the upside is enticing. With such a big potential payoff, it is hard to completely ignore it. So a majority of publicly traded REITs, have, at one time or another, owned or developed raw land, although no REITs engage in that activity as a prime source of income.

The REITs that have owned raw land use it for buying and selling, which in turn (they hope) leads to short-term cash gains.

Hotels/motels

This sector is one of the more risky ones when it comes to actual buildings, primarily because it is so dependent on economic cycles. For example, in the weeks and months after the September 11, 2001, terrorist attacks, when the national economy was at a standstill and travel was even slower, the hotel/motel market felt the prickliest pinch.

Hotels and motels can be broken down into various sectors. These include luxury, business-travel-centric, mid-market, and economy. Another sector, with its own breakdowns, are bed & breakfasts and independently run inns. Historically, hotels and motels have also been key cogs in boom and bust cycles, a problem exacerbated by overbuilding at high times of a real estate's market cycle.

Further adding to the risk level is that real estate bedrock, location.

Even more micro-based, if the hotel is off a highway, what else is nearby, such as restaurants and gas stations? How easy is the highway access? For beachfront properties, location is micro, too. How many rooms have windows facing the water?

There is also the state-of-the-economy factor. In one sense, this factor has a daily/nightly reach on the hotel industry. Room rates can, and do, go up and down on the economic cycles, which, again, are predicated on demand. The higher the demand, the more a hotel charges for rooms, while lower demand brings the prices down.

This factor can be seasonal, such as the difference in prices for hotel rooms in Florida in say, August and January. Another factor could be the part of the country the hotel is in: a mid-priced hotel in New York City might go for $350 a night, for instance, which could be a luxury rate in Nebraska.

There is, thankfully for real estate investors, some good news. Hotels and motels, despite the multitude of questions and high-risk quotients, have one attribute not often found in business: a control factor. Managers, both individual and from a corporate perspective, can do a lot (or a little) to improve (or damage) a hotel's vitality. This can be through adjusting rates higher or lower to stay competitive, as well as adding amenities, such as room service, a pool, and other recreational activities to enhance the guest experience.

All of that control is a key factor in determining a hotel's customer brand image and reputation. That factor, in this business, is big in determining long-term sustainability and profitability. Think about the last trip you took and how much impact a hotel's brand name and image had on you and your family's decision to stay there or look elsewhere.

Self-Storage Facilities

Put this under the category of "We should have thought of this first." The entire industry is built around the concept that, collectively, we have too much stuff and need a place to store it because we can not fit it in our houses. Self-storage centers fill that need, literally and figuratively.

It all adds up to some hefty numbers: As of late 2007, the United States' self-storage industry had a market capitalization of more than $220 million and $22.6 billion in annual revenues, according to the Self Storage Association, an industry lobbying group. That money comes from 51,000-plus self-storage facilities, which cover more than 2.2 billion rentable square feet, the association says.

Therefore, there is moneymaking potential in the industry. On a case-specific level, there are other advantages, too. Self-storage facilities are easy and inexpensive, relatively speaking, to build. Materials cost less, for one, and it is essentially building the same garage-like structure many times over.

A key component of building a successful self-storage facility is the location; putting one no more than five miles from a highly populated area is essential. Furthermore, a location near several middle-income apartment complexes, where people tend to run out of space more quickly, would be even better.

The self-storage industry, initially developed in the 1940s and 1950s as a way for transient military personnel to store belongings, has prospered along with the country's population — and stuff — boom. In the early years, though, many self-storage operators were looking to put something on land that could lead to some short-term revenue. After a few years, the thought was, the owners and developers could then put something more significant and lucrative on the land.

It turns out though, that self-storage operators discovered the margins, at least in well-located and well-run facilities, were good — good enough to be competitive with other real estate holdings. This realization led to even more growth in the industry.

Still, all of these positive attributes being said, there are some lingering risks in the self-storage real estate sector. These factors include short-term leases, heightened competition due to the low costs and low barriers to entry, and a constant need for qualified, sometimes 24-hour managers.

Shopping Centers

Following self-storage facilities with shopping centers in a breakdown of the types of real estate makes perfect sense. People need places to buy stuff that they need to store.

The shopping center landscape, though, holds some stark contrasts to the self-storage industry, or for that matter, nearly any other industry. For starters, there is the sheer size of it: about 200 million Americans visit some form of a mall or shopping center every month, numbers that can get even higher during heavy shopping seasons, such as the holidays or back-to-school times.

The United States has more retail space per person than any country in the world, and as such, many books have been written on the challenges and struggles of running a successful retail center or store.

Large-scale retail is made up of three categories: shopping malls, which are made up of super-regional malls, regional malls, theme malls, specialty malls, and discount or outlet centers; shopping centers, which include strip malls, mom-and-pop stores and community-based outlets; and freestanding retail, which can be composed of so-called "big-box" retailers, such as Wal-Mart or Home Depot, as well as regional chain stores.

Like any real estate category, location of a retail center, be it a Wal-Mart in the middle of Nebraska or the enormous King of Prussia Mall in suburban Philadelphia, is integral. Outlet centers, for example, tend to be located near high-population areas and are easily accessible from major highways.

But beyond location, the relative quality of the stores in a center goes a long way toward determining its quality as a real estate asset. The top-tier tenants are commonly known as credit tenants, and they tend to be national, or at last regional, in scope. Many are publicly traded, with access to capital.

These credit tenants — department stores such as Nordstrom's, Macy's, and Saks Fifth Avenue — are a boost to shopping centers in several ways. The stores tend to be a customer magnet, which in turn boosts the image of the whole facility and also gives it a leg up in attracting other sought-after credit tenants.

So it follows, naturally, that a retail project with several high-level credit tenants will be labeled as a Class A property, while a property with lesser-quality tenants will be classified as a class B property.

For real estate investing, as well as REITs, this designation is key, because the class and structure of the stores are an integral factor in determining rental rates, which is how a shopping center makes (or sometimes loses) money.

The risk factor in shopping malls stems from competition, as the sheer number and variety of shopping centers, combined with the typical fickleness of the American consumer, leads to uncertainty about which project will be a hit and which one will fail.

Office

This sector, in some ways, could be as wide-ranging and diverse as retail. Size, style, and focus of office buildings and complexes cover a wide range. Also, an analysis of offices as real estate properties includes industrial properties, too, as many companies combine the pair.

As such, the list of challenges is long when it comes to owning, maintaining, and developing office/industrial sites. This includes predicting demand for certain types and locations; keeping the properties up to date, both in a physical and technological way; and factoring in the changing needs of a variety of tenants.

Those factors, combined with the high number of investors and property owners who have a stake in these properties, help make this already-cyclical sector volatile, too.

Office properties, and the rents its owners can charge, go by a basic, subjective class-structure philosophy: individual properties are put into Class A, B, and C classifications, and landlords can charge accordingly. Just like in many other real estate sectors, the age of the building, its location, and its features go a long way toward determining its class designation.

Class A properties are defined by their high-end features. That includes using high-end building materials, designing a unique and sometimes flashy interior layout, and providing top-shelf amenities inside the actual offices, such as video-conferencing capabilities or Wi-Fi Internet capacity for the entire building. Class A properties bring the highest rents in the sector, but all also tend to have the most expenses.

Class B is the standard downgrade from Class A, similar to a fading Hollywood movie starlet. The building is still functional and provides several solid attributes, but the market is going other places. Class B properties tend to be built as a Class A facilities and then over the years deteriorate into class B designations. Price-wise, this sector provides the biggest challenge for office space owners and landlords. That is because Class B landlords cannot realistically charge the highest rents, like Class A owners can, but it is also too expensive to be attractive to tenants looking for something rock bottom.

That rock-bottom category is reserved for Class C. Those buildings tend to be converts, which is a building built many years ago for one use that is being turned into offices or a combination of office/warehouse. The buildings in this category tend to have few amenities and no marketable features.

The class structure is subjective, designed by the real estate industry as a guide for buyers and sellers. Naturally, a buyer would say a building is a "B" to bring down the price, while a seller would say it is an "A." Landlords and tenants play the same game. Also, some commercial real estate brokers have altered the class designations to include highs and lows within each letter, so maybe a building that is good but not top of the line could be a "low-A."

No analysis of office as real estate would be complete without mentioning location, because, like with anything else in real estate, that factor is crucially important. That goes for tall office buildings downtown in big cities, as well as for suburban office parks. Determining a quality location for office parks is one area where it is important to sweat the details and the little things that make a big difference, such as having a Starbucks in the lobby.

Residential

Even with the housing ownership boom of the 1990s and early 2000, the apartment and multifamily real estate sector has continued to grow, to the point where, in 2007, the total value of the apartment industry nationwide was valued at more than $2 trillion.

Apartment buildings tend to be anything with five or more units in a single building, while multifamily housing signifies buildings with four or fewer units.

From a rent-charging perspective, apartment complexes tend to be labeled under the same class categories as office buildings, with similar subjective reasons for saying one building is Class A and another building is Class B.

Beyond the class ranking, apartment complexes can be broken down into five categories: Low-rise, which are normally three stories or less and built in attached-townhouse style; mid-rise, which are defined more by location than height, as a mid-rise building in Sarasota, Florida, might be a low-rise in a bigger city, such as Miami; high-rise, which tend to be 10 stories or greater, especially in big cities; infill, which are built on small land parcels in highly populated urban areas; and garden, which tend to be sprawling complexes with low- and mid-rise buildings that are built with features such as pools, tennis courts, and clubhouses.

Affordability, or lack thereof, is the biggest factor facing investors when seeking long-term profitability and sustainability in the apartment and multifamily sector. This relates well to the classic rent-or-buy argument many individuals and young families face. It's not surprising, then that affordability, in terms of renting or owning, is driven partially by location.

Some areas with exceedingly high home values, such as Northern California or Long Island, New York, force a segment of the population into renting, as the costs of buying outstrips their financial means. (An exception to this rule, of course, has been the nationwide mortgage meltdown era of the 2000s, when many former renters who could not afford to buy a home from a long-term perspective indeed bought a home anyway, thanks to interest only and other creative mortgages.)

In areas with high home prices and, thus, a flush apartment renting market, the challenges again fall back to quality and location. On the former, amenities are especially key, and not just in pools, tennis courts, and gyms, which have grown to become givens, not necessarily special features, in many apartment complexes.

Renters are now looking for high technology, such as Wi-Fi Internet access and top-tier cable-ready television capabilities. Although more features draw more potential renters, they also add to a landlord's/owner's expenses, which, in turn, affects the return on the investment.

The Big Picture

Looking at just those six types of real estate can be overwhelming. Making things even more complicated is that the industry continues to grow and evolve, adding even more subsectors and property designations.

It is also important to recognize some of the risks and potential worries when investing in any type of real estate. For instance, real estate's lack of liquidity is often cited as the biggest negative factor in any real estate portfolio. This is because the buying and selling process of real estate can be complicated, sometimes taking up to six months or a year to close a deal.

That is not like selling shares of Coca-Cola. That takes little more than a phone call with a broker, or in some cases, a few mouse clicks.

Also, as with many of the properties described above, real estate, like politics, is inherently local. So buying and selling properties in more than one market requires not only an evolving education, but much patience as well as diligence.

Again, selling shares of stock in a company is a far less complicated process: a stockbroker will take an order no matter where the investor is physically located, be it Kalamazoo, Michigan, or Kansas City.

In terms of investing in any real estate property, it becomes a personal call depending on personal circumstances. For example, how long is the investor planning to hold on to the property? Is it a long-term investment or something flipped for short-term gain? Within that question, an investor also needs to have an honest assessment of his or her risk tolerance.

When things are looked at under such a big-picture view, investing in real estate is similar to getting into REIT investing. The next chapter will attempt to answer some of those REIT-specific questions that arise.

3

The ABCs

If property location was a constant theme of Chapter 2, then consider accounting principles to be the ongoing theme of Chapter 3. That is because REIT investing includes some accounting issues and terminology that are specific to REITs.

To be sure, there are some investing principles that apply to REITs, too. For starters, there is the basic "buy low/sell high" axiom, which is parallel to "location, location, location." That theory holds that the best way to make money in the market, and in REITs, is to build a portfolio based on a few principles and then keep it for years and years. It's hoped, the saying goes, you bought it for a low price and will be able to charge a high price when selling it.

In the stock market, one myth of this idea is the "watch it grow" part so often associated with it. At least, that aspect has been mythical the last few years of big fluctuations in the stock market.

With REITs, however, the buy-and-hold strategy works a little better. If you have put together a blue-chip portfolio of REITs, you can theoretically put it in the proverbial back corner and "watch it grow." In the case of REITs, at least over regular stocks, this is made possible, even lucrative, because of the annual dividend REITs are legally required to provide.

But this book, and specifically, this chapter, aims to assist REIT investors seeking to outperform the market. To get there, it pays to first define some accounting and economic principles and how they relate to REITs. These principles, some of which are unique to REITs, will be integral throughout the rest of this chapter and book as a guide for REIT investing.

The key terms include:

- **Net asset value (NAV)** refers to the commonly accepted market value of a company's assets and properties after subtracting its liabilities and obligations. Based on their structure, REITs are one of the more popular investment vehicles to be judged on a net asset value basis; as such, a REIT's NAV is a popular and important tool.

  Still, in the view of some investors and analysts, a NAV tool is important, yet incomprehensive. That is because some investors hold the view that a REIT's market value is not only based on property assets, but on the total business package, too.

- **Funds from operations (FFO)** is the net income a REIT generates, excluding gains or losses from sales of property, and adding back real estate depreciation. When compared to normal corporate accounting, it is a good approximation of cash flow and considered to be an even better judge of operations than the standard for United States public companies: generally accepted accounting principles (GAAP).

Although FFO is the most commonly accepted reported measure of REIT operating performance, the problem is that the industry has yet to develop a standard, uniform method for it, so it can be hard to use when comparing REITs to each other.

• **Adjusted funds from operations (AFFO)** is used by analysts and investors to measure a real estate company's cash flow generated by operations. The standard method for this calculation is twofold. First, it subtracts the REIT's FFO from normalized recurring expenditures that are capitalized by the REIT and then amortized but which are necessary to maintain a REIT's properties and its revenue stream. That includes items such as new carpeting in apartment units and leasing expenses. The second facet for calculating AFFO is to subtract what is known as the straight-lining of rents from the FFO (see below). A REIT's AFFO is also known as a cash available for distribution (CAD).

• **Straight-lining** is a calculation derived from the average of a tenant's rent payments over the entire lifetime of the lease. REIT accountants and financial executives incorporate straight-lining into their record keeping process because it is required by generally accepted accounting principles (GAAP).

• **Cash (or funds) available for distribution (CAD or FAD):** Besides counting as a REIT's AFFO, CAD refers to a REIT's ability to generate cash and to distribute dividends to its shareholders. This point is especially pertinent to the lifeblood of REITs, as the ability to generate a consistent dividend is both what makes a

REIT what it is and what attracts many investors to it in the first place.

CAD or FAD is derived by subtracting nonrecurring expenditures from a REIT's FFO, on top of subtracting normalized recurring real estate-related expenditures and other non-cash items.

- **Positive spread investing (PSI)** is a common way for any public company to manage its risk and in the process earn a rate of return that exceeds its capital costs. For a REIT, PSI involves "the ability to raise funds (both equity and debt) at a cost significantly less than the initial returns that can be obtained on real estate transactions," according to the National Association of Real Estate Trusts (NAREIT).

  The contribution of funds to generate the PSI normally comes from three areas: investment yield, capital costs, and rate of activity. Investment yield refers to how much money a company receives from a certain investment, either its return on costs or its return on assets. The more risk a company takes on in the front end, the higher the returns can be in the back end. The question REIT operators debate is how much risk to take, especially with other opportunities in the marketplace to generate investment yield.

Next up in the positive spread investing equation is cost of capital. To create the spread, the capital costs have to be less than the yield. This is where a company's balance sheet comes into play, as well as credit and equity markets. Companies with lower debt rate, for instance, tend to have better credit, and, it follows, access to a higher ratio of corporate debt. High-growth-rate companies, conversely, tend to have lower equity costs due to having high earnings multiples.

Finally, there is rate of activity, the final component of positive spread investing. This determines how long the PSI will last, based on how many investments a given company can make going out as long as three or even five years.

- **Cash yield on cost (CYC)** is a company's net operating income, or a company's operating property revenues minus operating expenses. When used properly, it is a good measurement of a company's return on assets or the money it has invested in a given property.

- **Weighted average cost of capital (WACC)** is the weighted average of a REIT's debt and equity costs. In practice, the WACC is the formula for how cash flow determines a company's net present value (NPV).

  The WACC of a REIT is a crucial measurement for investors. If a company's WACC projects a positive cash flow looking ahead, then that is a sign of a good investment. If the cash flow, or the net present value, is projected to be negative, based on the WACC projections, then the investment likely has weak potential.

- **Umbrella partnership REIT (UPREIT):** Essentially known as an operating partnership, this is when the partners of one structured company or REIT team up with the principles of another, newer REIT. For their respective interests in the operating partnership, the partners from the older REIT contribute the properties, while the new REIT contributes the cash proceeds from its public offering.

According to NAREIT, the REIT is the general partner and the majority owner of the operating partnership.

But there is more upside to an UPREIT. According to NAREIT, after a given time, often one year, the partners are allowed to have the same liquidity of the REIT shareholders by selling their pieces of their partnership for either cash or REIT shares. What is more, there is this, according to NAREIT: "In addition, when a partner holds the units until death, the estate tax rules operate in such a way as to provide that the beneficiaries may tender the units for cash or REIT shares without paying income taxes."

So much for death and taxes.

- **DownREIT:** This is the younger brother of an UPREIT. Indeed, a downREIT is structured in essentially the same way as an UPREIT, only in this case the REIT owns and operates properties under a separate partnership.

- **Dividend reinvestment programs (DRiP):** This is an underappreciated and, in some case, underused aspect of REITs. For any company, a dividend reinvestment program is when the company directly offers an investor the opportunity to pass the quarterly dividend back to the company.

  But this is not a charity case. The investment return from the dividends can be used for price appreciation and compounding without incurring brokerage fees. What is more, DRiPs allow investors to take advantage of dollar cost averaging with the income — the corporate dividends — the company is paying out. This way, an investor gets the return of the yield as well as the potential of stock gains.

What a DRiP is not, however, is a way to avoid taxes. Those must be paid on dividends, whether taken straight up as cash or put back into the company through a DRiP.

- **Cap rate**, formally called a capitalization rate, is a method of determining a commercial real estate property's risk level. A cap rate is determined by dividing a property's post-expenses net operating income by its purchase price. The higher the cap rate, the higher the return potential, as well as the risk. The lower the cap rate, the lower the perceived risk.

  So, a property with an annual net operating income of $100,000 and an asking price of $1 million would have a 10 percent cap rate. (Net operating income is the total cash flow a property produces before paying down debt.)

- **Equitization:** This term describes the process of how a tangible asset, such as real estate, is divided up among several investors and placed into publicly traded stock. In some accounting principles, it also allows the parent company of the entity to calculate the net income of subsidiaries on a monthly basis and then increase the investment, if necessary, before consolidating properties and assets.

- **Leverage:** This describes the amount of debt in relation to either equity capital or total capital. In real estate, just like in any other financial investment, more leverage means both a greater risk and a greater potential payoff. If an investment carries a high margin or leverage, it holds that it will carry higher risk, as even a small decline in the asset's value will wreak havoc on the entire investment.

From Theory to Practice

The trick in REIT investing is to devise a strategy where the alphabet soup-like definitions come together to help an investor understand and then improve his or her REIT investing performance.

Well, there is no one clear-cut method, which can be both overwhelming and helpful. Overwhelming, because there is much information to absorb, but helpful, because different valuation models and options can lessen an investment's risk.

Because a REIT, at its core, is a publicly traded company, a good place to start is to examine the components of valuation in any publicly traded entity. There are three big ones: determining the hows and whats of the entity's cash flow, trying to gauge the company's expected short-term and long-term cash flow, and figuring out the price to pay for shares.

The nature of a company's cash flow — its revenues minus its costs — is the most important part of the equation. For a REIT, costs can be operating expenses, administrative costs, financial costs, and capital expenses. Specifically, those costs could be anything from leases to new drapes in an apartment or new carpets for an office to debt payments.

A REIT's FFO is the most widely used and accepted method for determining earnings, as other measurements do not always take real estate-specific features into consideration. For example, a real estate's net income can be hard to gauge, as frequent property sales and leverage can inflate and distort the deprecation deduction. This is more than a few pennies, since many real estate properties appreciate in value over years, especially during high-inflation periods. The funds from operations measurement eliminates this volatility by excluding property sales and property depreciation.

The accounting method used to determine FFO does not include real estate depreciation, but it does include property capital expenses, tasks that help a REIT manager keep a property competitive in the marketplace. These costs are important to recognize when studying a REIT's finances, because it presents a clearer picture of the amount of capital available for distribution (CAD). That, in turn, makes it easier for investors to compare companies owning a variety of properties.

For instance, take two REITs, one operating apartments and another managing office properties. If the office property REIT has lower capital costs — maybe the buildings are newer and need less upkeep — then that means it will have a higher rate of capital available for distribution and thus, more cash for investors' pockets.

In addition to more cash, a higher CAD rate means the REIT will trade at higher levels.

Before any cash is available for distribution, though, there has to be revenue. The sources of revenue can vary based on what type of property the REIT focuses on; apartments are different from hotels, which are different from office parks.

A REIT balance sheet does not break out revenues on a line-item basis, but there are several revenue staples, including:

- **Rents:** The most basic form of generating revenue a REIT can engage in. Otherwise known as a lease, the trick is to raise rents at a level where the value is still appreciated by current and future perspective tenants. Those rates are determined by a number of marker valuations, such as inflation or location of the building compared to competing properties. Good old-fashioned negotiation tactics play a role in setting lease rates, too.

- **Percentage rent:** This revenue stream stems almost exclusively from having tenants in retail. Known also as a breakpoint, it allows the landlord, or, in this case, the REIT operator, to receive a prenegotiated amount of cash from the retailer if it reaches a certain point in sales. This concept is of the "you scratch my back, I will scratch yours" philosophy: the landlord agrees to do things — at his own cost — to drum up business for the retailer, such as signs, advertising, and promotional events. In turn, the retailer kicks back a percentage of the sales.

- **Lease and management income:** Sometimes, REIT companies become the outsource firm, managing and running other properties for a predetermined fee. Normally only the bigger REITs, with several departments, use this revenue stream.

Other REIT revenue sources can include fees from parking lots, vending machines, and other building components. Some REITs earn interest on cash balances held in bank accounts.

Operating expenses take the biggest bite out of a REIT's revenues, similar to the financial operations of any company. Just like revenue streams, the sources and amounts of revenue expenses can vary, depending on the actual type of property a REIT runs.

These are five of the most common and costliest operating expenses a REIT will have:

- **Utilities** tend to be the most volatile expense a REIT operator will face, as changing seasons and weather determine how much heat or air conditioning needs to be pumping. The bigger the building, the more costly energy bills can be, although managers of shopping mall-based REITs will attempt to get lower per-watt costs due to the bulk of the energy needs.

  Hotels tend to have high utility costs, as there is no system (at least none has been discovered yet) for charging hotel guests a fee for running the heat, the TV, and all the room lights. Some apartment-based REITs mitigate some of the utility costs by passing the expense on to the tenants.

- **Maintenance/upkeep** costs tend to be less volatile than utilities, but they can also be more expensive. In a high-rise office building, for instance, the costs could include elevator maintenance and outside window cleaning. And the bigger the square-footage, the more it costs for internal upkeep, such as pest control and maid service. Building size affects mall and shopping center-based REITs, too, as keeping lush landscapes is an important, yet costly, endeavor.

- **Marketing/promotion** expenses can be one of the most difficult for REIT operators to figure out, solely because marketing results are so difficult to determine. For example, was it the big billboard seen off the highway that led to increase in traffic at a given mall on a dreary Saturday afternoon, or were people going to come to the mall anyway? Should an apartment-based-REIT manager take out ads for vacancies in a daily newspaper or look for less costly Internet-based advertising? REIT managers, at least, can take solace in knowing that marketing costs are tough to figure out for nearly any businesses owner and entrepreneur.

- **Property taxes:** The taxes REIT owners pay on property controlled by the trust can be wildly different from year to year, state to state, and even town to town. Although property taxes take a big chunk out of any REIT's operating expenses budget, the actual amount can fluctuate based on several factors, including the sale price of similar buildings nearby and the appraisal policies of the governing area. The latter factor can be especially volatile, as is anything where politics are involved.

  Although not a REIT, Wal-Mart, the world's biggest retailer, attracted national business news coverage for its property taxes in 2007, as the company looks to be more aggressive in fighting high property tax costs in some areas of the country.

- **Insurance:** The cost and relative volatility of paying for insurance depends mostly on location. Nearly every

REIT, no matter the building focus, will have some combination of fire and personal liability insurance, which, on an annual basis, is fairly predictable and on the lower end of the insurance cost structure. REITs operating and controlling buildings in hurricane, high-flood, and earthquake-prone areas, however, face a more costly and volatile insurance plan.

Administrative, financial, and capital costs make up the rest of the REIT cost equation. The administrative costs refer to the overhead it takes to run the company, from salaries for the top executives to other staff members, to internal office rent and equipment costs. Writing, printing, and distributing communication materials for potential investors and shareholders, items such as quarterly and annual reports, also fall under the administrative cost domain.

Financial and capital costs are also integral to a REIT's cost structure, as real estate is one of the most cash-intensive businesses in existence. REITs, just like most other companies, access capital in a variety of ways, with a focus on short-term debt, used mostly for purchase; long-term debt, which can eventually be used to pay off short-term debt; and selling shares of stock.

The Net Answer

The big question lingers: what method can investors use to decide if a REIT is right for them?

There is no consensus among REIT managers, shareholders, and financial advisors about how to answer that question. In many ways, that makes it like the stock market, where there are countless ways — some proven, some not — to try and make the Next Big Investment.

Still, going back to a term defined at the beginning of the chapter is a good place to start. That term is net asset value, or the market value of a company's assets and properties after subtracting its liabilities and obligations. This works because the NAV system, at the end, helps an investor figure out if the REIT stock is trading at a discount or a premium in regard to its assets, as well other stocks.

One caveat to this theory: determining a REIT's net asset value is not always an easy process, despite the wealth and breadth of research data available to REIT investors today. The calculation is not listed in a REIT's financial statements, and furthermore, from a company-policy perspective, most REITs do not figure out the NAV anyway. Interested investors can play financial detective, though, and try to determine a REIT's net asset value on their own; sources include a combination of brokerage house research reports, which sometimes perform their own NAV analysis, in addition to commercial real estate brokers and a REIT's investor relations department.

But in basic terms, since many REITs, especially the big ones, own buildings in several different geographical areas, the first step in determining a REIT's net asset value is to take its net operating income out of the equation. What is more, REITs rarely disclose net operating income on a per-building basis, so it makes sense to apply a cap rate to a REIT's entire real estate portfolio.

The cap rate for the REIT takes several facets into account, beginning with the potential depreciation of a property over time and ending with insurance and risk issues. An up-to-date debt ratio is also included in this calculation, as is sector of the stock market, building location, expenses, shareholder's liquidity, and balance sheet strength.

In the end, the goal is that figuring out a REIT's net asset value will give the potential investor an idea of what a fair trading price is. So, if the net asset value analysis determines a REIT should be trading for $30 a share but it is going for $23 a share, then the investor has a potential good buying opportunity. If, on the other hand, that same REIT trades at $34 a share, it is likely overvalued.

From net asset values to more traditional stock-picking methods, the values of REITs have played a big role in the asset's topsy-turvy history. Chapter 4 goes into more detail about the life and times of the REIT industry.

4

Real Estate Investment Trusts: A History

Real estate investment trusts are about 50 years old. Like just about anyone turning 50, the REIT industry can look back at its first half-century of existence and see a variety of experiences that got it to where it is today.

In some periods it was hard to understand what the outside world was doing, such as the first few years; other periods were bleak and confusing (teenage years, anyone?), and still others were marked by growth and maturity. There have been some good years financially, and then there have been others, that, well, were not so good financially.

Finally, as the REIT turns 48 in 2008, it can look toward its next 50 years with the comfort and security of having come this far and in doing so, creating a legacy that can last into generations.

But before looking at REITs on a decade-by-decade basis, it pays to look at REITs' ancestors. There is a small amount of disagreement as to how exactly a REIT was started.

One account has it that REITs date back to the trusts and robber barons of the 1880s. Back then, trusts were not taxed at the corporate level, according to Richard Imperiale in the book *Getting Started in Real Estate Investment Trusts*. By forming a trust, then, investors were able to avoid being taxed if they distributed the income to the trust beneficiaries.

Over time, this tax advantage was eliminated, according to Imperiale, the founder and president of the Uniplan Cos., a Milwaukee, Wisconsin-based investment advisory firm focusing partially on REITs.

Other analysts and REIT historians say the origination of what we now know as a REIT today stems from wealthy residents and deep-pocketed investors of early 1900s Boston. It's fitting, in a way, that the city where residents famously protested taxation without representation may turn out to be the place where the tax benefits of owning a REIT were initially developed.

The story goes like this: the industrial revolution put much money into a few people's hands, which led to a demand for real estate investing opportunities.

But state laws prevented budding real estate moguls from owning real estate through a corporation unless the property was essential for the business to function. So a corporation in Boston could not buy a building for purely investment or redevelopment purposes.

The Massachusetts Trust changed all of that. Formed by some wealthy individuals in response to the laws of the day, the trust was an avenue to legally allow companies to invest in real estate for non-business functioning purposes.

Trust benefits included perks corporations received, including limited liability, unified management, and employee control as well as the ever-important tax benefits. Through negotiations and agreements with the federal government, the Massachusetts Trust legally was allowed to remove federal taxes, which in turn allowed the trust operators and real estate owners to reinvest money into other properties.

This concept, originally designed for wealthy investors and landowners, soon made its way to the not-so-rich around Boston and Massachusetts. The concept had legs outside New England, too, going as far as cities such Chicago, Denver, and Omaha, Nebraska.

A pair of late 1920s/early 1930s hurdles, though, put up a significant blockade toward future growth of the then-fledgling real estate investment trust concept. One hurdle was the Great Depression, where food on the table took precedence over lowering taxes on real estate investing.

The Massachusetts Trust — and the REIT concept — was hit even harder in 1935, when the U.S. Supreme Court ruled that the trusts were not exempt from corporate taxation structures.

That court decision ultimately left REITs competing with actual regulated investment entities, such as closed-end mutual funds that were created by the Investment Company Act of 1940. Without the tax benefits to offer potential REIT investors or operators, the concept drifted into obscurity.

By the 1950s, though, there were some sign of life coming from the REIT respirator. REIT advocates started lobbying federal congressmen to write legislation that would put trusts on the same taxation ground as mutual funds.

The original legislation that created mutual funds and REITs have many similarities. The list includes limitations on the type of income each entity is allowed to focus on; mandated distribution of taxable income; and, at least in 1960, both mutual funds and REITs were subject to a 90 percent income distribution clause.

The lobbying efforts paid off in 1960 when President Eisenhower, just a few months before his presidency was to end, signed the Real Estate Investment Trust Act into law.

The 1960s

The REIT industry jumped out of the gate like a thoroughbred, galloping to just under $300 million in total capital raised within the first two years. Just like predecessors of 60 years earlier, most of those initial REITs were seeking opportunities in real property and land. These were the initial equity REITs.

But, sticking with the horse racing analogy, within two years, REITs had slowed to a trot. The culprit? The stock market free-fall of 1962. Capital in any section of the market quickly diminished, and by some accounts, the REIT industry grew by only about $70 million over the next four years.

It was not only the stock market slide of the early 1960s that led to the early demise of REITs. Despite the fight just to get the law passed, REITs were not exactly a household name in those early years. Many investors, both individuals and institutions, stayed away due to a lack of understanding of the benefits of the investment structure.

Financial records show that by 1965 there were fewer than 65 REITs in operation, with many of those predating the 1962 stock market slide. What is more, according to "The REIT Investment Summary," an industry report published in the 1996 by the Wall Street investment firm Goldman Sachs, only about ten of those 1960s REITs were significant in size and reach.

The operators of those REITs outsourced the executive management functions of the trust, as well as the property management responsibilities. This structure is no longer used, as the split leads to a conflict of interest for the REIT owner/operator, one where the investor can easily end up on the short end.

Despite the growing pains, there were some stars of the 1960s REIT time period. For example, one of the first official REITs, Real Estate Trust of America, held about a $45 million portfolio throughout most of the 1960s, a large sum of money for the time and the industry. The owners of Real Estate Trust of America were part of the initial group of lobbyists that initially pushed for REIT legislation.

Furthermore, even though the stock market was riding a jittery roller coaster for most of the 1960s, the real estate market was doing quite well. The Goldman Sachs report shows that cash flow among REITs of the 1960s grew an average of 5.8 percent a year, while the average dividend yield was 6.1 percent.

Investors seemed to respond better to the investment vehicles as time passed on to the 1970s. For example, between 1968 and 1970 REIT assets grew more than four times, from about $1 billion to about $4.7 billion.

REITs' return record of the 1960s proves that the appreciation was mutual between investor and investment fund: from 1963 to 1970, REITs produced an average annual total return of 11.5

percent, a solid return that shines even brighter when put up against the S&P 500's average annual total return of 6.7 percent during the same time period, according to the Goldman Sachs report.

One other key point of the first decade for REITs can be seen in the up and down changes in the type of investment trust that dominated the market. In the early post-REIT Act years, most REITs were essentially equity REITs, focusing on standard property investments funded with stock equity and other investment capital.

But cash flow levels became more important to shareholders as the decade moved along, and by the late 1960s, REIT operators responded by relying on short-term borrowing to meet and exceed margins.

This change had the effect of moving several REITs into the mortgage arena and away from being pure equity investments. Indeed, between 1968 and 1970, just fewer than 60 REITs were formed — an unprecedented boom period — and just about every one of those was a mortgage-based REIT. This change in structure also gave birth to what today is called the hybrid REIT.

In addition to investor demand, there was another force pulling REITs from the equity side to the mortgage side. That magnetic force started with the Federal Reserve Board, which, in an effort to reduce inflation and jump start the nation's sluggish economy, raised the interest rate in 1968.

The rate increase, while succeeding as a national economy boost, could also be placed on the shelf of unintended consequences. That is, banks, thrifts, and S&L operations were put in a bind with the rate hike, as those institutions were bound by other laws as to how much they could raise their rates. Lenders at those same institutions were also restricted in their ability to loan money to construction and development companies due to more government regulations, a problematic facet of the economy that would not fully show itself until the 1970s.

Mortgage REITs, already getting a boost from investor demand, were the beneficiaries of the federal rate hike. In 1968 alone, three mortgage REITs hit the market in a big way: that year, Republic Mortgage Investors, Associated Mortgage Investors, and General Mortgage Investors raised nearly $75 million in public offerings, almost 70 percent of the entire industry at the time.

The boom reverberated into the next two years, as in 1969 the REIT industry hit the billion-dollar mark in new shares, while in 1970 it raised about $1.3 billion.

The 1970s

In several pronounced ways, the 1970s were not too good to REITs, at least that was the case with the then-booming mortgage REIT side of things. From an economic perspective, the 1970s were not too good to many people: inflation, OPEC-driven fuel shortages, and high unemployment rates were the norm, not the exception.

But in the beginning of the decade, the construction and building industries were rolling, and so too were REITs. Office buildings were being planned and built in record time.

While this was going on, banks, S&Ls, and thrifts — up until then the traditional lending sources for construction companies and developers — were having some problems enjoying the good times. In addition to government regulations and interest rate hikes, those institutions were facing yet another cause-and-effect problem: the rate hikes put the institutions in a situation where their ability to raise funds for any loan was severely restricted by paying higher rates on deposits.

Mortgage REITs, however, easily filled that void in the early years of the 1970s. Mortgage REITs, by definition, must place at least 75 percent of their holdings in mortgages and short-term loans, so in a sense, the government-endorsed structure of a REIT was the key for the growth period. What is more, since the rates REITs paid out were not regulated, the REIT operators had few problems paying the higher interest rates necessary to finance the somewhat more risky construction and development loans.

Some of these newly formed mortgage REITs were set up by offshoots and units of those same jilted financial institutions. Banks got into the game at this point too, and, just like previous economic booms, there was much blind following going on. Bank of America, Wells Fargo, and Chase were among the legions of banks to sign on the mortgage REIT dotted line in the early 1970s.

In the beginning, the results, on paper at least, were stellar and dramatic: by the middle part of the decade, REIT assets had jumped to the $20 billion-plus range, an enormous leap in such a short time.

Now, for the bad news. Most of these REITs were top-heavy. They were structured with little shareholder equity and many borrowed funds to provide the construction and development loans.

By 1973, when the bottom started falling out of the previously booming office building industry, REITs' problems grew even worse. Many REIT operators found that leverage — the amount of debt in relation to equity or total capital, a calculation that was once their ally — could be used against them, too. It did not help that during the boom period, investors and analysts later discovered, underwriting standards were shoved to low priority status, in an effort to out-bid competitors.

Unfortunately, investors, executives, and even REIT owners and operators do not always heed history's lessons. Consider only the most recent example: the residential mortgage-lending debacle that played out nationwide in 2007, one that was marked with similar lack of underwriting principles.

Nonetheless, the 1970s were not a total REIT meltdown. This was made entirely possible due to equity REITs, which were able to maintain profitability and even grow as a result of using low leverage levels and conservative investment theories and techniques. Asset growth might have slowed among these REITs, but the returns and operating performance were solid, even besting the S&P 500 again.

As good as they were, however, equity REITs alone could not rescue their industry. Part of that job fell to the federal government — not always a sure thing.

The government's answer was the Tax Reform Act of 1976. On the one hand, the law had some positive attributes, and it provided REITs some breathing room to adjust to sudden and then long-lasting economic downturns. Curiously, at least from the perspective of REIT operators — or maybe not, as this was, after all, a government operation — the 1976 law increased the dividend payout requirement to 95 percent from 90 percent. That rule went the opposite way in providing REITs a cushion from earnings losses.

The government gets an A for effort but a C as far as results go. Moreover, judging strictly with a numbers perspective, things were not nearly as good for the REIT industry as the decade ended. Some numbers: total REIT assets dropped from $20.4 billion in 1974 to $7.1 billion in 1981, according to published reports. The total number of REITs, both public and private ones, dropped, too, from 250 in 1972 to 124 in 1982.

Compounding the problem was that REITs were going through an industry-wide image problem. The mortgage REIT debacle occupied most of the business news headline space. And the fact that a majority of investors did not differentiate between mortgage REITs and equity REITs, at least when it came to actual dollar allocations, did not help matters.

The bottom line? By the end of the 1970s, the REIT industry's market capitalization was as low as it had been since 1972.

The 1980s

The REIT industry began to recover in the 1980s, as did the real estate market. Still, the period goes down as one of the more tumultuous in REIT history.

From a market perspective, escalating mortgage rates, which at times went as high as 13 percent and 14 percent, were problematic for REITs. Borrowing costs went up with the mortgage rates, and FFO growth slowed considerably.

Not that REITs were suffering too much — they were buoyed in part by low supply of office space and apartments, which, in turn, led to higher rental rates.

The numbers looked good. Between 1981 and 1984, for example, average total capitalization among all publicly traded REITs rose 119 percent, while returns climbed 92 percent. According to Goldman Sachs's REIT report, FFO growth in the first half the decade grew, on average, more than 8.5 percent per year. The average annual return rate between 1980 and 1985 — 28.6 percent — was an even better gauge for how well REITs were doing.

Volatility, though, was looming.

From a macro perspective, the volatility could be traced to two bills passed by Congress: the Economic Recovery Act of 1981 and the Tax Reform Act of 1986.

The Economic Recovery Act at first proved to be beneficial to REITs. The problem was that over time, the act gave birth to new market players, in addition to giving institutions such as banks a fresh piece of the real estate pie.

Features of the economic recovery legislation included providing investors several tax breaks through operating loss pass-throughs and trimmed-down depreciation schedules. Investors were able to use these breaks as a way of reducing personal income tax liabilities.

Hello, boom times. About the same time as when the bill's ink dried, a new industry sprang from what was once the domain primarily of REITs. A plethora of limited partnerships were formed to take advantage of these tax breaks, and the partnerships raised more than $80 billion during the 1980s, considerably more than REITs did.

These Economic Recovery Act-induced partnerships were a concoction of banks, loan institutions, and brokerage firms. The vehicle for the investment was called a real estate limited partnership (RELP).

These RELPs had several advantages over REITs. First, the limited partnerships took on more leverage than REITs and as such could provide greater returns. The increased tax write-off possibilities were another plus.

What is more, RELPs were designed to sell for less than their net asset value, which, the theory went, would lead to a quicker sale. That limited shelf life, in turn, would make sure investors would earn capital gains shares when the property was sold and the RELP was terminated.

In the land of American taxation law, however, all good things come to an end sooner or later. About RELPs, that time was sooner. Five years after the Economic Recovery Act of 1981, Congress passed the Tax Reform Act of 1986.

This law curtailed most of the previously described tax breaks, giving REITs a better seat at the table, again. Many saw that as a good thing, too, as real estate market valuations had grown skewed with the large amounts of tax-break motivated capital coming into the picture.

The law also tinkered with the original 1960 REIT Act, such as modifying REIT ownership rules.

Specifically, the 1986 legislation allowed REITs to own and operate most types of income-generating commercial properties, the former being a responsibility that previously had been outsourced to independent third-party companies. This change had the effect of allowing the financial interests of REIT operations and managers to merge with REIT investors — something previously seen as a conflict of interest. That conflict, right or wrong, had long been a reason investors shied away from pumping significant amounts of capital into REITs.

Long-term, the changes imposed by the Tax Reform Act of 1986 would prove to be as good as gold for the REIT industry. Short-term, not so much. The 1980s, according to the National Association of Real Estate Investment Trusts (NAREIT), saw the reversal of the two-decades-strong trend that had REIT returns beating the S&P 500; in the 1980s, the S&P 500, on a total annual compound basis, beat REITs by a few percentage points.

The 1990s

The Tax Reform Act of 1986 had some long-lasting legs. Indeed, the 10 years after its passage, especially 1992 to 1997, represented the greatest boom period REITs had ever gone through.

For instance:

- The total number of REITs in 1990 stood at 67. By 1995,

that number had nearly tripled, to 179, and by the end of the decade the total number of REITs had passed 200.

- The average capitalization for all REITs, at least the ones publicly traded, went from $72 million in 1990 to $252 million in 1995 to $726 million by the end of the decade.

- As an industry, REITs' market capitalization levels skyrocketed in the 1990s, from less than $15 billion when the decade began to more than $800 billion when it ended.

The boom, though, could be traced to more than the federal government's tax reform act. One catalyst for the boom was that REITs performed so badly in 1990 that they became a bargain, even for those not considering REIT investing. The bear market was so, well, bearish, that REITs' total return for the year was 14.8 percent, according to the National Association of Real Estate Investment Trusts. Since 1974, REITs had only been in the red, on a return basis, once, and that was in 1987 when it was down less than 4 percent.

The bear market was, looking back, quite typical of downturns. Many REITs cut dividends to bring in expenses, and investors responded by dumping REITs, a constant cycle. Some markets and sectors, such as office properties, were still in the middle of an overbuilding era, and that did not do much to improve either the REIT industry's financial numbers or investors' confidence levels.

But 1991 turned out to be the year of the backpedaling bull. In addition to simply a buying frenzy brought on by cheap stock prices of 1990, investors and financial observers give credit to one company in particular for the turnaround, Kimco Realty.

Kimco, coincidentally, was founded in 1960, the same year the federal government passed the REIT Act. But back then, friends and partners Milton Cooper and Martin Kimmel were shopping center developers in south Florida.

Kimco had grown significantly by 1990, and company executives were seeking even more growth, which would require substantial access to capital. So the company launched a public offering on November 22, 1991, a move that would go on to be a seminal moment for both the company and the REIT industry.

The IPO raised $128 million — pittance by the standard of late 1990s tech company IPOs but a windfall to a 1991 REIT. It was the most money a REIT had raised in an IPO in more than three years.

Beyond being a source of capital for Kimco, the company's REIT lent some much-needed credibility to the REIT industry. The company came to the publicly traded REIT world with a solid track record and has since grown even more, further rewarding investors. By the end of 2007, Kimco controlled more than 1,500 properties nationwide, making it one of the largest publicly traded owners of neighborhood and community shopping centers in the United States.

If it can be said that Kimco gave REITs a friendly push, then it seems as if more government regulations and legislation, as well as investors that were fueled by yet another building boom, gave REITs a forceful shove.

Investors, primed by investment bankers eager to capitalize on fees from a previously untapped IPO market, were key to what is commonly referred to as the early 1990s REIT IPO boom. And booming it was: in 1993, for example, REIT public offerings raised $18.3 billion, followed by $14.7 billion in 1994, according to NAREIT.

Plus, the IPO boom, in addition to providing investors and REIT operators with a fresh pile of cash, also served to open the doors to other parts of the property industry. No longer were REITs satisfied with simply owning a few small-scale strip malls and apartment buildings. Indeed, the early 1990s is when equity REIT managers started expanding property portfolios to include a variety of sectors, including offices and hotels.

Some of the more recognizable names from the blue-chip REIT roster — Kimco, Duke Realty, and Simon Property Group, to name a few — were all launched in one way or a another during the 1993 to 1994 REIT IPO boom.

The boom, though, was short lived, and the second half of the decade, while a net gain, was quite tumultuous. It virtually went bear-like for two years, followed by two years of bull activity, followed yet again by two years of a bear-like atmosphere.

Then, in 1999, the federal government stepped in with one of the most significant pieces of REIT legislation since the original REIT Act of 1960.

The latest piece of legislation was called the REIT Modernization Act of 1999, and among other features, it allowed REITs to own up to 100 percent of a taxable REIT subsidiary (TRS). This new ownership feature allowed REITs to provide services to tenants without jeopardizing the status of the parent REIT — no small distinction, one that the industry would still be absorbing nearly a decade later. The legislation also altered a 1980 provision by reinstating the original rule of requiring REITs to distribute 90 percent of total income back to shareholders; the 1980 law had upped the distribution requirement to 95 percent.

The 2000s...and Beyond

In some ways, the past decade of REITs has been a continuation of the 1990s roller coaster, with some good years followed by some not-so-good years. The key, though, at least from REIT supporter standpoint, was that REITs gained major strides in investor acceptance.

The first half of the decade was an especially good one for REITs, even more so considering it took place during the post-September 11, 2001, stock downturn and the tech stocks bubble burst that dragged down the entire market. With an average annual return of 22 percent for the 5 years ending December 31, 2004, according to NAREIT, the REIT sector overwhelmingly beat the NASDAQ (-6.7 percent loss) not to mention the S&P 500 (-0.7 percent loss).

Return ratios continued to fluctuate the next three years, but within REIT supporter and investor circles there was one constant: optimism. Looking at the next 30 years, it is not uncommon to see analysts predicting 10 percent a year growth within the entire REIT sector.

These gaudy predictions are made, in part, based on the several positive attributes a REIT provides, a list that includes management accountability to shareholders, liquidity, and a low-leverage method of owning real estate. Nonetheless, as you will see in the next chapter, there are several myths and misunderstandings that threaten the growth of the REIT sector.

• 5 •

REITs on the Street

Until now, this book has focused mostly on what a REIT is. That is, the parts that make the REIT tick, from its legislative requirements, to its checkered history, to some of the more specific calculations used to determine a buy or sell order.

It is also worth looking into what a REIT is not. Specifically, what are the myths and misunderstandings in the investment community about REITs? The problems start with pronunciation, mistakes even made by so-called experts.

Ralph L. Block, one of the most renowned and well-known experts in the REIT industry, addressed and then debunked several of these myths in his book *Investing in REITs*, now in its third edition. In addition to publishing the newsletter *The Essential REIT*, Block has been on the inside of the industry as a portfolio manager and on the outside as an investor and shareholder. The National Association of Real Estate Investment Trusts (NAREIT) presented Block with its 2004 Industry Achievement Award.

The sheer popularity of REITs — $450 billion in assets spread over more than 200 publicly traded entities makes it more than a bit player — shows that there are some people out in investor-land who have seen through the myths. Still, it could be bigger, and by most expert predictions, it will be bigger someday soon.

One account for the slow and scattered growth is not a myth as much as it is a misunderstanding. Indeed, just the word "trust" can lead to problems. Beyond that, REITs were caught in investor no-man's land: pure real estate investors and commercial brokers did not want to be bothered with a stock market product, and stock market investors wanted the next Google, not a piece of ownership of a mall in St. Louis or an office park in San Antonio.

Those two groups hesitated to come out of their comfort zone and take the leap.

Real estate executives, for example, had plenty of things going for them by simply being in real estate. Depreciation costs allowed the real estate investor to generate a tax deduction, and leverage, especially in a thriving market, provided further profits and investment opportunities. For those reasons and others, real estate investors figured they were better off owning and investing in the actual real estate as opposed to buying stock certificates that could make them one of hundreds, if not thousands, of owners.

Then there were the investors — the institutions and the individuals. From an institution standpoint, REITs were mostly a novelty, as big funds tend to be driven by investing in stocks and funds with high liquidity rates, thus decreasing the risk factor. Up until the mid-1990s, though, the common perception was that there was not enough liquidity in the REIT market to bring in big institutional investors.

Many individual investors also suffered from not properly understanding the REIT investing concept. To start with, the concept of buying and selling shares of a company that is in the business of owning, renting out, and selling buildings, from apartment skyscrapers to shopping malls, was in of itself, foreign. Better off sticking to oil companies, banks, or car companies was the prevailing thought in many individual investing circles, the whole "stick to what you know" philosophy.

Another problem was the mutual fund misunderstanding. Because REITs are essentially big bins of smaller parcels, many investors assumed a REIT was a boring, low-risk, low-return mutual fund. REITs were not even called into the S&P 500 until 2001, and many analysts, including Block, cite the mutual fund misconception as part of the reason for the delay. In 2001, the federal government officially signed off on REITs as an active business, further distancing the investment vehicle from mutual funds, at least publicly.

It did not help matters that one of the leaders in the misunderstanding department was the brokerage community. Up until the mid 1990s, few firms had a team of stockbrokers and analysts that truly understood the REIT investing structure, and even fewer firms employed analysts for the sole purpose of analyzing REIT stocks, as opposed to beverage companies, airline, or tech stocks.

Put together, these misunderstandings had the cumulative effect of forming a Catch-22 between real estate investors who consider REITs only for stock market investors and stock market investors who consider REITs only for real estate investors.

As the case with just about anything in life, misunderstandings, left alone to linger along enough, tend to become myths. Some of the now-disproved myths include:

REITs are riskier investments than "regular" stocks, as proven by the sector's sometimes poor showing during slowdowns and slumps in the real estate industry.

This myth can otherwise be classified as saying that bad news for real estate investors will ultimately end up translating to bad news for REIT investors. It is just that, a myth.

First, a glimpse at the numbers. According to the NAREIT Equity Index, REITs' worst performing year since 1980 was 1998, when they produced a -17.51 percent return. A wretched year, to be sure, but by 1999 the loss was trimmed to less than -5 percent, and by 2003 it was in the plus 40 percent range.

The late 1990s were indeed slow times for commercial real estate, as overbuilding in the office market was leading to a slowdown in several markets nationwide. However, the real estate market has suffered through other downturns since 1980, yet REITs, on a numbers basis, did not suffer in lockstep with the market.

Well-managed and well-run REITs can survive, even thrive, in poor-performing real estate markets. For example, sometimes, unfortunate as it might be, one tenant's foreclosure or bankruptcy could be another REIT's buying opportunity.

Even REITs' worst years, from a return perspective, were not nearly as bad as how some other sectors and indices have fared from time to time. Tech stocks took a dive in 2000 after the bubble burst, for example, but by 2006, people were buying tech stocks again. Airline stocks, too, suffered significantly in the months and years after the September 11, 2001, terrorist attacks.

Yet today, some investors are buying tech and airline stocks, making the decision on the merits on each actual company, not the fortunes (or misfortunes) of the entire industry. REIT supporters are doing the same when it comes to REITs and rough real estate markets.

A housing market slump will drift to the commercial sector, sooner or later.

The last explanation attempted to disprove the supposed connection between a bad commercial real estate market and the REIT industry. Still, investors, from time to time, have been scared away from the REIT market due to a residential real estate down cycle.

Housing slumps, which indeed can and have triggered tough times in the commercial real estate industry, rarely make a significant difference to REITs. For starters, the commercial rise and fall cycles tend to be less volatile than its residential counterparts.

What is more, high mortgage REITs could lead people away from buying a home and into renting an apartment, which could be a good thing for an apartment-based REIT.

REITs are on the low end of performance ratios, at least when compared to other investments on the market.

This myth was covered in Chapter 4, which saw the rise of REITs over the last 45 years, as compared to the market. The National Association of Real Estate Investment Trusts weighs in further on the issue, stating that from the mid-1970s through 2005, REITs have not only outperformed both the NASDAQ and the S&P 500, but they have done so with considerably less volatility.

What is more, REIT returns have a low correlation when compared to other sectors, further disproving the myth. In responding to just this myth of the REIT industry, NAREIT Senior Vice President of Investor Outreach Michael Grupe said, "We often talk about REIT stocks offering both bond and stock attributes. Their return characteristics tend to fall between those of other stocks and bonds. These characteristics are what lead to the stock's important diversification benefits."

REITs are risky because the product is commercial real estate, which is a risky investment.

Real estate, in itself, is not necessarily the risk, but instead it is how the portfolios and properties are managed, from both a financial and a physical, hands-on perspective. This includes facets such as diversification, leverage, and the quality of the fund managers. The latter, the people running the REIT, go a long way to determining how good (or bad) the entity's diversification and leverage are.

For example, a commercial property owner (or a REIT), that has properties only on earthquake-prone areas of Northern California is obviously being overly risky. It would make sense to have a portfolio with more diversification, such as buildings in another part of the state or country.

The theory of diversification is commonly preached in the investing community. No stock broker worth his Series 7 license would tell an investor to put all his money in one or two stocks. Although some investors choose to put more money one place than another, nearly every portfolio is diversified, at least to some degree.

Well-run commercial real estate portfolios are heavily diversified, further disproving this myth.

Finally, a word about risk. Every investment carries some sort of risk; even choosing to put money into bonds over stocks is, at its core, a risk. Leverage, though, is how investors in any sector, including commercial real estate, hedge against risk. The more leverage, the greater the risk. That is not a commercial real estate related phenomenon.

REITs are pass-through companies that merely hold real estate properties for periods of time before selling.

Although this could be true, this is a severe misunderstanding of REITs, if not a full-blown myth.

To be successful or even to be sustainable, a REIT, by definition, has to be a well-managed, proactive, and entrepreneurial company. REIT managers have to be aware of multiple markets, the opportunities and the dangers both, and be ready to act decisively when a quick decision is needed. REIT executives, be it for strip malls, self-storage facilities, or hotels, also have to develop coherent business strategies and then make sure the staff is in place to properly execute the plan.

REIT stocks are beneficial only for short-term trading, and investors can get out at any time.

This statement is inherently mythical, just as it would be if the word REIT was replaced by oil and energy company stocks or beverage company stocks. Primarily, this is because there are not any stocks built for short-term trading that can be easily sold for big profits.

Sure, it is possible to make money in the markets this way, even using REITs. But it is impossible to time the market, both when a downturn has hit bottom and when a boom has peaked. That type of activity is speculation, not investing.

As detailed in this chapter and earlier in this book, the REIT sector has outperformed many other sectors and industries. Therefore, even if an investor were inclined to go short-term on some of his portfolio, it would likely be a mistake to choose REITs as that vehicle.

What is more, there is at least one big reason to hold on to REIT stocks longer than even other stocks: dividend. REIT stocks, by law, pay back a dividend every year to investors. Although other companies pay back dividends as well, those are not guaranteed and sometimes are not as lucrative.

The REIT industry has spent considerable time attempting to dispel these myths and other misconceptions the investment community has about REITs. Some efforts have been successful, one of the many factors responsible for the industry's recent growth. Other myths linger.

Even international REITs have spent time combating some of

these myths. For example, London-based Hammerson (**www. hammerson.com**), a REIT with properties in England and France, has a myth/reality page on its Web site. The company's effort, a good example of what other REITs have had to do to get the message across, is essentially a beginner's primer on what constitutes a REIT.

A Street Fight

The next logical step in the analysis of how REITs perform in comparison to other investments would be to examine how the stocks perform long term, or at least how they do after the IPO phase.

The key part of this examination, just like it would be for any other experiment, is the makeup of the study group. In many ways, this analysis is even more pertinent for potential REIT investors then the previous probe into IPO returns because the specific characteristics of the study group narrows the comparison.

For investors seeking to gauge how REITs perform when put up against other investments, it is essential to use a study group made up of stocks that are built like REITs. This list, what is known as a relevant market list, should therefore be made up of high-yield stocks with low volatility, less risk, and small capital appreciation. Big growth stocks need not apply.

In practice, this list includes preferred stocks, bonds, utility stocks, and sometimes convertibles.

Pitting REIT stocks against utility stocks is one of the more common comparisons. Research and anecdotal evidence over the last 15 years has shown that when utility-based stocks suffer, due to factors such as deregulation, too much regulation, or good old-fashioned competition, investors have moved some money over to REITs. The thinking goes that investors can still get some of the same benefits of utility stocks through REITs, namely a high dividend.

However, that has not always been true the other way around: when REIT stocks struggled for a few two-year periods during the 1990s, investors did indeed dump REIT stocks. Only there is not much evidence of investors moving that money into utility stocks. That could be one reason to choose REITs over utility stocks.

Another factor in the REIT versus utility stocks comparison is future prospects. It can be reasonably argued, for example, that utility stocks — companies such as Duke Energy Corp., Exelon Corp., and FirstEnergy Corp. — are already well known and well understood by the investment community. That is not to say that those stocks cannot or will not grow or that they are not capable of outperforming REITs. Utility stocks, though, do not have the same upside potential that REITs do. (How many books are devoted solely to the education of investing in utility stocks?)

REITs, on the other hand, have a much greater chance of bringing in new investors — and not just because there are more books on the subject. The upside potential rests on the idea that since REITs have been regularly misunderstood; once investors "get it," they will back it up with money.

The comparison between REITs and bonds and, to a lesser extent, preferred stocks, is not as straight up apples-to-apples like the utility stocks comparison. First off, bonds and preferred stocks, the latter of which has a fixed dividend but is not part of the company's total portfolio in that it has no voting rights, will always pay off a yield.

That is not the case with REITs. Sometimes REITs can have problems that cause it to drop its REIT status. And not having a REIT status means there will not be any dividend. Kansas City-based subprime home lender and mortgage REIT NovaStar Financial, Inc. giving up its REIT status, detailed in Chapter 1, is just one example.

The flip side in the comparison, though, is that bonds and preferred stocks have limited growth potential, unlike REITs. Indeed, preferred stocks, by definition, do not provide a payoff when shares increase or a loss when shares decrease.

This brings the conversation back to the risk-versus-reward scenario. That is, REITs might have more risk than bonds, but REITs also have a chance for a more substantial return.

Plus, the prices of bonds and preferred stocks tend to fluctuate heavily in accordance with interest rate movement. That is not the case with REITs.

The fight pitting REITs versus convertible stocks and convertible bonds could be the most even comparison. Convertible stocks and bonds, which are issued by companies to potentially provide an ongoing stream of income for investors, can bring both a high yield and appreciation potential.

The problem, though, is that a company issues convertible stocks and bonds at its own discretion. So it is not as if an investor can just buy and sell convertibles whenever he wants to, like he can with REITs.

Investing in REITs, however, goes deeper than a comparison to other investment vehicles. The next section of this book indeed attempts to go deeper, with an examination of the REIT sectors an investor can choose from. This examination includes looking into the history, makeup, and strategy of more than 30 actual REITs.

CASE STUDY: CHRISTOPHER R. LUCAS

Senior Research Analyst

Managing Director

Robert W. Baird & Co.

www.rwbaird.com

As the director of research for a national organization designed to support REIT companies and investors, Chris Lucas witnessed the frenzied growth of the REIT market in the late 1980s and early 1990s.

No more so than while eating lunch.

That is, when Lucas first started out in his position with the National Association of Real Estate Investment Trusts (NAREIT) in 1987, he could take a leisurely lunch have no phone messages on his return. But in 1991, after Kimco's $128 million public offering, Lucas says he could come back to his desk and have 50 messages waiting for him. Lucas said, "The growth of the industry was phenomenal."

Today, Lucas tracks the industry from the perspective of a research analyst for Milwaukee-based financial services firm Robert W. Baird & Co.

CASE STUDY: CHRISTOPHER R. LUCAS

Based out of McLean, Virginia, Lucas covers mostly industrial and retail REITs, in addition to companies that focus on East Coast office space. He also travels nationwide to Baird's offices to talk to the company's financial advisers about the REIT market.

One ideal Lucas promotes is to avoid "commodity markets or products" when investing in REIT stocks. Lucas is referring to staying away from a REIT that owns anything related to the commodities markets. A commodity market is essentially one with little barrier to entry and as such risks having unconstrained supply side. That leads to heightened competition, which can squeeze a REIT's profits and dividends.

Suburban office space in the Southeast United States, says Lucas, is an example of a REIT-based commodity market. There is so much of it already, and relaxed zoning requirements in many cities and towns means there will always be more.

As of early 2008, Lucas said two REIT sectors with defensive investment characteristics that held promising potential were healthcare and triple net lease REITs. In healthcare, the country's aging population virtually assures that the industry will continue to grow. And, says Lucas, triple net leases, when executed properly, have a large potential upside.

6

Office REITs

Office REITs are one of the most, if not the most, volatile sectors of REIT investing. It makes sense when considering the risk-heavy, topsy-turvy nature of the trillion dollar-plus office real estate industry itself.

For REIT investing purposes, it is one of those high-risk, high-potential-reward scenarios.

The risks themselves are a combination of boilerplate real estate and macro-economic challenges that include figuring out job growth trends with pinpoint accuracy; closely monitoring supply-and-demand ratios; and, maybe the toughest challenge, constantly dealing with the customer base, a diverse group of demanding tenants.

As with most things in life, though, the challenges themselves might be boilerplate, but the heavy lifting is in the details. Tenant demands, for instance, vary widely, from size and location requirements to the particulars of what each company needs in an office. Keeping properties up-to-date is the key, especially when it comes to technology, such as having high-speed Internet connections.

One caveat to any discussion about office REITs: in REIT-speak, office-based investment trusts are sometimes lumped together with industrial space-based REITs. That is because often, prospective tenants need both industrial/warehouse and office space. Also, the office and industrial sectors are just about the only aspects of the real estate industry where the primary clients are other businesses.

Still, the histories and dynamics of the office and industrial/warehouse sectors have several differences from an investment standpoint. Hence, this chapter will focus primarily on office REITs, and another chapter will delve into industrial REITs.

As of the end of 2007, office properties nationwide, from city skyscrapers to rural one-level buildings, were valued at about $1.1 trillion, a number stemming partially from an industry building boom that lasted almost all of the 1980s. About 20 percent of the total office properties in the country are corporate-owned entities, with no relevance to the REIT market.

The remaining 80 percent, or roughly $850 billion worth of office properties, are considered investor-owned — either individually or by a group. Of that 80 percent, about 10 percent, or $100 billion, are owned by REITs, according to the National Association of Real Estate Investment Trusts (NAREIT).

It is a small piece of the office property pie, but it is a big pie.

According to NAREIT, as of November 30, 2007, there were 15 publicly traded office REITs, a number that does not include either straight-up industrial REITs or any combined office/industrial REITs. Office REITs represent about 15 percent of all publicly traded equity REITs and have a market capitalization of about $40.17 million.

Property, Property, Property

Office properties are split into five size-based categories, with exceptions factored in for some of the biggest cities, such as Chicago, Philadelphia, and New York, where big, at least compared to other cities, is relative. The categories include high-rise buildings, which are at least 15 stories tall; mid-rise, which are more than three stories; low-rise, which are three stories or less, built next to each other in row-house style; office parks, which tend to be large-scale suburban-built sprawling complexes; and flex, which are combinations of industrial and office space.

The height of a building is particularly important when it comes to office property investments, as height goes a long way toward determining a building's cost and long-term expenses.

High-rise and many mid-rise buildings, for example, tend to have the highest cost factor. For starters, there is simply more space, which means more upkeep and maintenance responsibilities. Beyond that, the buildings tend to be in urban areas, where land is scarce and more expensive. Low-rise and office parks tend to be built on land that does not cost as much as it does in urban areas.

The expense factor is integral in attempting to achieve long-term success in the office property market, and, it follows, office-based REITs. This is because the make-or-break point in office real estate is the rent a landlord can charge, and the higher the expenses, the lower the profit margins.

The category of office building is but one facet in determining an office rent. Another factor, and a big one, is simple supply and demand. That is, the less demand for space, the less a landlord can likely charge for space.

Other factors determine an office's vitality, too, mainly how the property is classified. As mentioned in Chapter 2, the real estate industry has a mostly subjective guide that designates a building as a certain type of property. Just like in school, there are top-of-the-line properties that warrant an A, down to average properties that receive only a C.

A building's age, location, and amenities are the main factors in determining its grade level.

Class A properties, which tend to be new construction in highly populated areas, are defined by high-end features, such as a high-end interior and technology features throughout the building. Although Class A properties can charge the most for rent, the expenses tend to be the highest in the sector, too.

A suburban office park complex is the standard type of Class B property: functional but fading in popularity. The rent structure of Class B properties tends to be the most volatile, as it falls in the classic middle ground: not good enough to charge top-dollar but not as far down the quality chain to be a rock-bottom bargain.

Class C properties, instead, fill that rock-bottom category. Class C buildings tend to be converts, better known as an old building that has been converted to office use, without many of the modern-day office building features.

The size, height, and class of an office building are just three components, albeit important ones, in determining the success of an office-property investment.

The supply-side factor is a significant component, too. An analysis of the supply dynamics of an office market starts with location, but it goes deeper than simply the street that the building is on.

From a prospective tenant's perspective, a desirable location has several factors, including how close the building is to an airport, its access to main roads and, in some cases, the availability of nearby public transportation. Other factors a prospective tenant might consider, all of which have an effect on the supply market dynamic, include the local government's business friendliness (or lack thereof), the customer base, and the local labor pool.

Then there is the point where supply and demand connect with each other: vacancies. This is the trickiest part of gauging the office real estate market, simply because of all the moving parts it has, many of which are moving at the same time.

For example, a market's vacancy rate includes some amount of sublease space, which is also sometimes referred to as shadow space. This is when a tenant has too much space, possibly because of a company downsizing or another market factor, and seeks to get another tenant to rent the underused space. This can be especially tricky, because in some cases, a tenant ends up competing with a landlord to rent out space.

New office space also plays a crucial role in figuring out a market's vacancy rates. Projects under construction and projects in the soon-to-be construction phase are essential to this segment of the market; prospective tenants might hold out signing a lease in one property to rent space in the newest property on the market.

Further adding to the volatility of the office sector are some long-term trends in the industry, beyond the complicated supply-and-demand factors. One major trend, which has been moving along since the building boom of the 1980s, is the growth of suburban office parks, at the expense of urban office locations. In many ways, this trend mirrors what has been happening nationwide to America's cities the last 25 years, as the big ones have been losing population to suburbs and so-called exurbs, which are themselves becoming small cities.

This trend is worth watching, especially for office REITs with holdings including downtown and office properties.

Another trend with the potential to affect the office market, one more recent, is telecommuting. Although millions of workers see the ability to work from home as a indispensable perk, one made easier through technological advances, the flip side is that it means fewer people are working out of offices. Fewer people in offices, long-term, could translate to a tenant requiring less space.

So, with all these pieces of the market moving at once, it should not come as much of a surprise that by sheer financial figures, office REITs have produced some of the most volatile returns in the market since 2000. A line charting the returns and yields would look something like an upside-down letter U, with an S scattered about: it started out bad, got better, and went back to bad, all with many ups and downs in between.

For example, from 2000 to 2004, the national office market was still dealing with absorbing the 1980s and 1990s overbuilding period. The glut of properties in multiple markets translated to a REIT operator's terror trifecta: little demand for properties, higher vacancy rates, and declining rental rates. By some accounts, the national vacancy rate from 2000 to 2003 doubled, to more than 15 percent, while rents dropped almost 5 percent.

Here is how that downturn translated to office REITs: in 2001, the sector produced returns of -0.8 percent, followed by an even more dismal -6.8 percent in 2002. The dividend yields dropped three straight years, going from 8.8 percent in 2000 to 7.7 percent in 2001 to 5.9 percent in 2002. Finally, the sector's estimated net asset value fell below the benchmark $100 million level, further cementing its well-deserved reputation for risk and volatility.

But by the next year, the glut began to dissipate and the bad times started to make a turn toward good times. In 2003, the sector produced a gaudy 34 percent return, followed by 23 percent in 2004 and an even gaudier 45 percent in 2006, according to NAREIT.

Still, the good times for the cyclical sector were not built to last. Indeed, in 2006 and 2007, the national vacancy rate was, for the most part, hovering at more than 10 percent — not a good sign for REIT investors. The results on the books again turned sour. For example, in 2007, the 15 pure publicly traded office REITs were down 18.96 percent for the year, while the average dividend yield was a meager 4.7 percent, according to NAREIT.

Individual Stories

Those numbers and analysis represent the full office REIT

spectrum. But individually, the companies that make up the nuts and bolts for the analysis and statistics tell a different story. Looking at these stories can help a potential investor make a decision about whether, or how much, to invest in a particular REIT.

Here is a glimpse inside four office REITs with distinct strategies and business models:

COMPANY: BIOMED REALTY TRUST

Ticker symbol: BMR; shares are traded on the NYSE

Web site: www.biomedrealty.com

Headquarters: San Francisco

Founded: 2004

CEO: Alan D. Gold

Revenues: $221.41 million in 2006

Market capitalization: $1.40 billion, as of February 23, 2008

Yield: 5.80, as of February 23, 2008

Properties: The company has 103 buildings spread over 68 properties, with 8.5 million rentable square feet of space and almost 2 million more square feet in the development stage. Cities the company has office space in include Boston, San Francisco, and Seattle.

Details: BioMed's niche is in providing office space for biotechnology and pharmaceutical companies, as well as scientific research institutions and government agencies involved in the life sciences industry.

The company, which was founded as a publicly traded equity REIT in 2004, is a fully integrated REIT in that it provides the management, leading, and development services for all of its properties. The company has full ownership stake in all of its holdings, with the exception of 11 properties where unaffiliated third parties also own interests.

COMPANY: BIOMED REALTY TRUST

The company, according to its Web site, says its long-term business strategy includes growing its high-quality office real estate portfolio in "high barrier-to-entry markets," a way of hedging against competition, not only from other REITs, but also from other commercial real estate developers. The company strategy also includes targeting assets with triple net leases, which, it says, "will enable us to manage a large property portfolio with a cost-effective management infrastructure."

Also, BioMed executives say they have several strategies for both internal and external growth. From an internal perspective, the plan includes leases that have built-in annual rent escalations, which, the company says, "provide us with predictable and consistent earnings growth."

Meanwhile, the company's external growth plan, in terms of buying and then leasing properties, revolves first around location. Specifically, BioMed is seeking property near academic and other research areas, prime spots for companies in the life sciences industry. The end game, the company says, is in developing long-term leases for perspective tenants, five to 15 years, with both the triple net and built-in rent escalations.

BioMed's cofounders, Alan Gold and Gary Kreitzer, held executive roles in two other property-based companies focusing on the life sciences industry before founding BioMed in 2004. One of those entities was Bernardo Property Advisors, a private enterprise founded in 1998 that focused on life science and medical facilities in the San Diego and San Francisco markets.

Gold and Kreitzer also were among a group of cofounders of Alexandria Real Estate Equities, a Pasadena, California-based company that, still operating today, is one of BioMed's chief competitors.

COMPANY: MACK-CALI REALTY CORP.

Ticker symbol: CLI; shares are traded on the NYSE

Web site: www.mack-cali.com

Headquarters: Edison, New Jersey

Founded: Cali Associates, primarily a homebuilding firm, was founded in 1949. Cali Realty Corp. initially went public as a REIT in 1994. In 1997, the company merged with the Mack Co., a family-run commercial real estate firm, also based in New Jersey, which was initially founded in 1962.

CEO: Mitchell E. Hersh

Revenues: $740.31 million in 2006

Market capitalization: $2.29 billion, as of February 23, 2008

Yield: 7.33, as of February 23, 2008

Properties: The company owns or has interest in 302 properties, mostly Class A office buildings in suburban markets in the Northeast United States. In total, the company has about 35 million square feet of space, occupied by a variety of 2,200 corporate tenants. The company also has an ownership stake in land adjacent to many of its properties that could be developed for more than 11 million square feet of additional office space.

Details: Mack-Cali's roots are in the sprawling suburbs of New Jersey, so it makes sense that as of 2007, the company was one of the biggest office landlords in the state. Other regions the company has had a presence in include Westchester County, New York; Fairfield, Connecticut; suburban Philadelphia; and suburban Boston. In 2007, the company ventured into big-city properties in a big way by buying a stake in a 40-story waterfront office tower in Manhattan.

The company's current strategy is to continue refining its presence in the Northeast through improvements to its current properties and new acquisitions, such as the skyscraper on 125 Broad Street in New York City. Indeed, as recently as 2006, Mack-Cali owned some properties in other parts of the United States, such as Denver and San Francisco, but by early 2007, the company had officially shed

COMPANY: MACK-CALI REALTY CORP.

all of its non-Northeastern United States properties.

The strategy also includes the selling of assets in the company's core markets where it is concerned the growth will be limited. For example, the company sold its only two office buildings in Atlantic City, New Jersey, in 2007. The properties "did not offer us competitive advantages or significant growth opportunities," Mack-Cali CEO Mitchell Hersh said in a November 1, 2007, letter to shareholders.

In terms of occupancy rates, the strategy seems to be working: going into the fourth quarter of 2007, the company's portfolio was 92 percent leased.

The company also has a role in a few high-profile development projects. It recently completed a 92,300-square-foot office building in Red Bank, New Jersey, that was constructed as a build-to-suit project and pre-leased for 10 years. As that project was being wrapped up, Hersh wrote in his late 2007 letter to shareholders, the company was also starting construction on a 250,000-square-foot office building in Parsippany, New Jersey, that hotel company Wyndham Worldwide has pre-leased for 15 years.

Finally, another large-scale development project the company is involved in is the $1.3 billion redevelopment of the Continental Airlines Arena site in East Rutherford, New Jersey. Mack-Cali is one of several partners on the project, which is designed as a 4.76 million square feet of family entertainment, office, and hotel space. The planned office component includes four 14-story buildings totaling almost 1.8 million square feet of space.

COMPANY: BRANDYWINE REALTY TRUST

Ticker symbol: BDN; shares are traded on the NYSE

Web site: www.brandywinerealty.com

Headquarters: Radnor, Pennsylvania

Founded: 1986

COMPANY: BRANDYWINE REALTY TRUST

CEO: Gerard H. Sweeney

Revenues: $662.80 million in 2006

Market capitalization: $1.45 billion, as of February 23, 2008

Yield: 10.53, as of February 23, 2008

Properties: Brandywine Realty Trust's portfolio consists mostly of Class A suburban and urban office space totaling more than 40 million square feet; about 29 million square feet of that space is run by the company on a consolidated basis. The company's holdings also include some industrial properties, in addition to some office/industrial combinations.

The portfolio is furthermore broken down into three geographical regions/strategic markets across the country. The company's biggest presence is in its Eastern United Sates region, which consists of properties in Delaware, Maryland, New Jersey, Pennsylvania, and Virginia. A second region, for the central United States, is made up of properties in Dallas and Austin, Texas, while a third market, for the West Coast, is composed of holdings in Oakland and San Diego.

In addition to the company's suburban Philadelphia headquarters, it has seven regional branches. Those offices are in Austin; Carlsbad, California; Dallas; Falls Church, Virginia; Mount Laurel, New Jersey; Oakland; and Richmond, Virginia.

Details: The company, one of the largest REITs in the office REIT sector, brings a diverse focus to a singular product style. The core product is Class A office space, while the focus includes working on all aspects of a transaction, including ownership, development, acquisition, and management.

That focus, according to the company's Web site, is broken down even further through a variety of development, construction, and building tasks the company's executives and personnel will undertake. That list includes several labor-intensive assignments, such as site selection, land purchase, deign and space planning, and construction management.

COMPANY: BRANDYWINE REALTY TRUST

The development process that Brandywine Realty Trust goes through with projects and clients is one of the firm's broadest and most well-known programs. Company executives consider the project management system a key strength of the business plan, and it has also been recognized as one of the most comprehensive approaches in the entire office REIT sector.

The project management system opens with a full-time project manager being assigned to meet weekly with the tenant. The project manager then expands the meetings and contacts to include consultants, local officials, and other people necessary to move the project along.

In addition, Brandywine Realty personnel will work with the large group of outside help necessary to complete an office building project, such as land-use attorneys, plumbers and electricians, traffic planners and engineers, and even an elevator consultant.

The project management system continues through both the pre-construction phase and the construction phase. In pre-construction, the company's project managers will assist with preliminary design criteria; help identify and receive local, regional, and state planning and zoning approvals; and establish a project schedule and a final schedule.

Then, in the construction phase, the Brandywine Realty project managers will continue to be involved intently in the project. During that phase, some of the tasks include assisting clients and tenants with cost control issues, subcontractor schedules, and quality and safety checklists.

Brandywine Realty Trust's project management system is being put to good use, too: as of early 2008, the company had $300 million worth of projects in its development pipeline.

COMPANY: PARKWAY PROPERTIES, INC.

Ticker symbol: PKY; shares are traded on the NYSE

Web site: www.pky.com

Headquarters: Jackson, Mississippi

Founded: 1971

CEO: Steven G. Rogers

Revenues: $215.34 million in 2006

Market capitalization: $534.95 million, as of February 23, 2008

Yield: 7.40, as of February 23, 2008

Properties: The company either owns outright or has an ownership interest in 66 properties in 11 states, mostly in the Southeastern and Southwestern United States, in addition to Chicago. The properties are composed of about 13 million square feet of office space. About 21 percent of the portfolio, or 18 properties totaling 2.7 million square feet, are owned jointly with other investors.

Details: Parkway's tenant list, which covers more than 1,500 clients, is diverse, including industries such as banking, insurance, legal, energy, and telecommunications.

Just as diverse as the company's client list, though, is its evolving strategy. Over the last ten years alone, the company has had three distinct business plans. Especially important to investors, the financial goals of the evolving strategies revolve around growing the company's funds from operations (FFO) to the point where the results are consistently exceeding those of its peer group.

Parkway's most recent mission is its GEAR UP Plan, which started January 1, 2006, and is scheduled to run through the end of 2008. The plan spells out some of the company's core goals: good people; equity opportunities; asset recycling; retaining customers; uncompromising focus on operations; and performance.

The mission: transform the company strategy from being an owner-operator to an operator-owner. Although the company will still provide fee-based real estate services through its Parkway Realty Services, the idea behind the transformation

COMPANY: PARKWAY PROPERTIES, INC.

plan is to capitalize on the company's strength in operation services.

Company executives consider the GEAR UP plan a natural transition from its VALUE^2 plan, which ran from 2002 to 2005 and was designed to focus employees on the operations side of the business. The GEAR UP program — at least the E and the A of the acronym — incorporates equity opportunities and asset recycling into the value strategy.

The equity phase, the company says, includes using both the public and private markets to seek out the best acquisitions and development projects. The asset part of the strategy focuses on selling off buildings and properties in markets that do not fit with the company's strategy of owning larger assets in institutional markets.

"These two goals," the company states on its Web site, "are what combine to transform Parkway from being first an owner of real estate and secondarily an operator of real estate for others to being first an operator of real estate for others that also owns an interest in the real estate."

Before VALUE^2 and GEAR UP, on November 1, 1998, Parkway had instituted what it called its 5 in 50 plan. The goal was to increase the company's FFO per share from $3.05 in 1998 to $5 a share in 50 months without issuing any new equity. The plan worked: by creating 17 action plans for various departments to work on, the company reached its goal of going over $5 a share in FFO.

7

Residential REITs

Apartments, the core product of a residential REIT, share some basic similarities to offices, at least in terms of a grading scale, building designation, and the tenant-landlord relationship.

Just like office REITs and their relationship with industrial properties, residential REITs essentially have a built-in subsector in manufactured homes. The manufactured homes REIT sector, however, is considerably smaller than its industrial counterpart is, and thus it does not warrant its own chapter of the book.

However, the biggest similarity between office REITs and residential REITs is in the final customer: people. Just as people will always need a place to work, so too will they always need a place to live.

That is played out in the growth of the apartment market nationwide. As mentioned in Chapter 2, even with the country's housing ownership boom of the 1990s and early 2000s, there has still been room for the apartment market to grow. By 2007, the total value of the apartment industry nationwide was valued at well more than $2 trillion.

In sheer apartments, that number is estimated to be in the mid- to high hundreds of millions, although a specific number is difficult to peg down, as the definition and scope of what makes up an apartment is more fluid than say, what makes up an office. This includes private homes and rooms above garages.

Still, analysts, looking at the entire residential REIT industry, claimed in 2007 there were about 1 million individual REIT-owned apartments, about 15 percent of the market and a significant leap from 1991, when the industry owned only about 50,000 apartments. Throughout the 1990s, many of those REIT-owned apartments were clustered, in that a residential REIT operating company tended to own apartments in the same geographical area, such as the Southeast or the West Coast. Some residential REITs have expanded their geographical reach in recent years.

Going into 2008, there were 15 pure residential REITs, the same number of pure office REITs, which represents about 15 percent of all publicly traded equity REITs. In 2007, residential REITs had a market capitalization of about $41.6 million, according to the National Association of Real Estate Investment Trusts (NAREIT).

For residential REIT purposes, apartment buildings tend to be anything with five or more units in a single building, while multifamily housing signifies buildings with four or fewer units. From a rent-charging perspective, apartment complexes tend to be labeled under the same class categories as office buildings, with similar subjective reasons for saying one building is class A and another building is class B.

The designations, too, are more for buyers and sellers of the properties, not necessarily potential tenants. Most residential REITs invest in Class A properties or at least stick to class B or better. Few, if any, residential REITs invest in Class C properties.

A Class A apartment building or complex is new construction or at least less than five years old. Its top-shelf features that separate it from other properties can include anything from a full-time concierge service to rooftop tennis courts to a courtesy car wash from the valet.

Class B properties tend to be older, and it follows, come with fewer star-quality features. Class C is the lowest grade on the apartment market, and the office market too, for that matter.

Again, like office buildings, apartment buildings also have designations based on a combination of height and physical layout. These designations include:

- Low-rise, which are built in attached townhouse style and are three stories or less.

- Mid-rise, which, strictly by definition are more than three stories high, but in practice, the category is location-based. For example, a 12-story building in New York City is a mid-rise, but the same height in say, Omaha, Nebraska, or Boise, Idaho, would be labeled a high-rise.

- High-rise, which are normally at least 10 stories tall, at least in heavily populated urban areas.

- Garden, which tend to be sprawling complexes with

low- and mid-rise buildings that are built with features such as pools, tennis courts, and clubhouses. These complexes tend to be built near shopping centers and offices and are popular with renters.

- Urban infill, which tend to be combinations of the previous designations and are built on small land parcels in highly populated urban areas. Sometimes these projects are public-private partnerships, or the developers receive some type of subsidy.

Although residential REITs have, and will continue to use all five of the property designations, the ones that have been the most popular have been the high-rise and garden variety. This is primarily because of density issues: both properties, at least the successful ones, tend to be good at packing the people in. The high-rise concept works well in the biggest cities, such as Los Angeles and Philadelphia, while the garden concept has succeed in smaller, yet growing cities, such as Jacksonville, Florida, and Charlotte, North Carolina.

Renting Versus Owning

The classes and designations, in many ways, have combined to produce a winning strategy for residential REITs. Over the last decade, the REITs composed of residential real estate holdings have produced some of the best returns in the entire REIT landscape. Through 2007 for example, residential REITs produced returns of at least 15 percent a year all but two years, according to the National Association of Real Estate Investment Trusts (NAREIT). That includes a stellar 25.5 percent in 2003, an eye-popping 35.5 percent in 2003, and 39.9 percent in 2006. (Not every year, however, as been a positive one for residential

REITs: in 2002, the sector was down 12.9 percent and as 2007 ended, it was down almost 15 percent for the year).

Meanwhile, the dividend yields from residential REITs on an annual basis have averaged anywhere between 6 percent and 10 percent, according to NAREIT.

Although the mostly stable and consistently stellar residential REIT returns are nothing to scoff at, the residential REIT sector does have some characteristics that make it tough to figure out at times, both in the short and long term. Many of these traits are paradoxical in nature, further adding to the confusion.

To start with, while the share prices of several residential REITs soared in 2004 to 2006, the yields suffered. Growth stocks do not normally produce big dividends in any sector, and, it turns out, that includes residential REITs.

There are other tug-of-war conflicts inherent to residential REITs, too, mostly in the rent-versus-owning battle. This plays itself out in many ways nationwide. A 2006 report released by investment banking firm Deutsche Bank comparing the costs of owning versus the costs of renting is a good starting point for examining how this fight impacts residential REITs.

The report devised a measurement tool for figuring out the cost owning a home through what it calls the ATMP, or after-tax monthly payment. It reaches the final figure by adding a potential homeowner's adjustable rate mortgage interest, property taxes, and insurance and then subtracting principal amortization and income tax savings.

The report then took those numbers to compare the average cost of renting an apartment to the monthly costs of homeownership in 47 metro areas across the United States. The results were tallied in a rent/own ratio for each market so, for instance, if the rent/own ratio is 50 percent in a given area and it costs $1,500 per month to own a median priced home, then a renter, on average, would be looking at paying about $750 a month for an apartment.

The rub lies in the fact that the ratio is rarely 50 percent. Indeed, in 2006, it was more like 35 percent or 40 percent in hot real estate markets such as those in Southern California, Las Vegas, or Southwest Florida. A lower ratio, the report projects, will translate into lower renting costs.

The question, then, becomes, "How are lower rental rates beneficial to residential REIT operators and investors?" The answer rests in the ever-popular supply-and-demand phenomenon. Consider it a domino effect: first, high home prices drive people away form buying into renting. Then, more renters put a squeeze on the supply, thus making apartments in more demand.

This rent-own theory has one major component that ultimately has the biggest say in a residential REITs success or failure: tenants. These are a residential REIT's only customers.

The bad news is that tenant turnover in the apartment business is high. Leases tend to run anywhere from six to 18 months, depending on the local market. Office leases, by comparison, tend to be for several years, sometimes as long as 10 or 15 years.

The short-term nature of the apartment leases can be costly for landlords, who need to be constantly updating and refining a marketing plan to keep the rental rates up. Other major costs for apartment landlords and residential REIT operators are in amenities — and not just tennis courts and pools, which have become so prevalent in some markets in recent years that they are almost a given. Instead, the amenities renters expect today revolve around technology, such as Wi-Fi Internet access and top-tier cable-ready television capabilities.

There are, however, some underlying good news factors for potential investors considering the apartment market. To wit:

- Cash flow tends to be both positive and predictable, as apartments tend to have a broad tenant base, such as 500 or 1,000 renters in a given property. When one, two, or even ten renters do not re-up their lease, the impact to the business is minimal.

Maintenance and upkeep costs are also minimal and predictable, as the apartments are essentially permanent, at least when compared to upkeep costs in either the hotel or the office industries.

- The industry, from an investor's perspective, is considered defensive in that people will always need shelter, so there will always be some sort of customer base. What is more, since apartment leases are short-term, they tend to mirror the current market forces and the real earning power of the property.

- Finally, the market for apartments is relatively predictable as compared to other property types. This is because most of the data used to project supply and demand, such as population demographics, job rates, and economic growth, can be easily found.

Individual Stories

Here is a glimpse inside four residential REITs with distinct strategies and business models:

COMPANY: CAMDEN PROPERTY TRUST

Ticker symbol: CPT; shares are traded on the NYSE

Web site: www.camdenliving.com

Headquarters: Houston

Founded: 1982

CEO: Richard J. Campo

Revenues: $580.58 million in 2006

Market capitalization: $2.71 billion, as of February 23, 2008

Yield: 5.67, as of February 23, 2008

Properties: As of the end of 2007, the company had 180 communities in its portfolio which were made up of about more than 63,000 apartments in 18 high-growth markets in the lower half of the United States. The locations spread across both coasts of the United States, from Washington, D.C., to Los Angeles, with stops in the Mid-Atlantic, Sunbelt, and Midwestern regions.

Details: Camden Property Trust's core operating strategy is wrapped around what it calls market balance. It is how the company looks for diversification in its properties and locations, which it achieves through a combination of acquisitions, developments, and mergers.

For example, the company says it achieved a goal of geographic diversity when it merged with Summit Properties in 2005. The merger gave Camden a footprint in four East Coast markets: Atlanta; Raleigh, North Carolina; Washington, D.C.; and Southeast Florida. In addition to reaching new markets, which aided the company's branding efforts, the move also allowed Camden to have its net operating income more evenly distributed.

The markets Camden moved into with the Summit Properties merger also represent one of the company's core concepts: going to

COMPANY: CAMDEN PROPERTY TRUST

markets that are leaders in population growth, household starts, and job growth — factors the company considers a priority in driving apartment demand.

The company was not always in the apartment business. When Richard Campo and his partner, Keith Oden, founded the firm in 1982, the original focus was on high-rise condo buildings. Within five years, the company had bought its first apartment community, in Houston, and in 1993, the founders took the firm public, looking to expand even more.

Since the 1993 IPO, the company has grown from a 300-employee company running apartment communities only in Texas to an almost 2,000-employee company with 63,000-plus apartments. Today, in addition to the apartment management division, the company consults with other firms looking to do a variety of apartment community-related activities, including construction, acquisitions, and redevelopment.

Camden Property Trust's financials have grown along with the company's portfolio over the last 14 years. Its stock price, for example, had more than tripled at one point, from $22 a share in 1993 to as high as $79 in 2007. (In early 2008, the company was trading in the mid-$40s-a-share range.) Its funds from operations (FFO) has grown from $1.86 in 1993 to $3.47 in 2005.

The company said it is also still in growth mode. Its development pipeline had more than $2 billion in current and future projects. After it completes 12 properties that were under development in 2007, it will have increased its portfolio to 66,000-plus apartments in 192 communities.

COMPANY: AMERICAN LAND LEASE

Ticker symbol: ANL; shares are traded on the NYSE

Web site: www.americanlandlease.com

Headquarters: Clearwater, Florida

COMPANY: AMERICAN LAND LEASE

Founded: 1986

CEO: Terry Considine

Revenues: $83.93 million in 2006

Market capitalization: $158 million, as of February 23, 2008

Yield: 4.96, as of February 23, 2008

Properties: The company operates about 8,000 operational home sites in more than the 30 communities across Alabama, Arizona, and Florida, with a focus on retirement communities. It also controls about 1,500 undeveloped home sites, 1,200 developed home sites, and 130 recreational vehicle sites in those states. On a total property basis, the company has about 72 percent of its properties in Florida, 23 percent in Arizona, and the remainder in Alabama.

Details: American Land Lease's mission is to be the leading developer and operator of manufactured-housing communities in the United States. By focusing on the retirement community, it hopes to capitalize on the needs of the country's much-coveted 55-and-over demographic.

The core of the business is running its residential land lease communities. Essentially, the company leases home sites to homeowners on large plots of land it owns. The communities are made up of subdivisions, each with central entrances, paved streets, and sidewalks.

American Land Lease then provides amenities for the entire community, such as a clubhouse, a pool, tennis courts, and a marina. The company also provides external services, such as lawn maintenance, trash collection, security, and maintenance of common properties.

In return for developing the community and providing the amenities and services, American Land Lease charges one-time and recurring fees from the homeowners.

In addition to developing and running the retirement communities, American Land Lease runs a home sales unit through a

COMPANY: AMERICAN LAND LEASE

runs a home sales unit through a subsidiary called Asset Investors Operating Partnership. This division is run like other homebuilding operations, with sales centers, model homes, and even custom-design capabilities.

The company's home sales unit suffered along with the rest of the country's slumping residential market in 2007. For example, it reported $7.2 million in home sales volume in the third quarter of 2007, a 41.3 percent drop as compared with the same time period in 2006. It reported 52 new home closings in the 2007 third quarter, including 49 new homes sold on expansion sites. That was 40 sales fewer than the 92 new home closings it reported in the 2006 third quarter.

American Land Lease is one of the publicly traded equity REITs that focuses exclusively on the retirement community. Another unique facet to the company is its chief executive officer, Terry Considine, who has been CEO and chairman of the company's board since 1996.

Considine, a 30-year veteran of the real estate industry, is a dual chief executive, as he also holds that title with Apartment Investment and Management Co., a Denver-based apartment REIT that runs 1,200 apartment communities in 46 states.

COMPANY: GMH COMMUNITIES TRUST

Ticker symbol: GCT; shares are traded on the NYSE

Web site: www.gmhcommunities.com

Headquarters: Newtown Square, Pennsylvania

Founded: 1985; company went public under current name in 2004

CEO: Gary Holloway

Revenues: $293.13 million in 2006

Market capitalization: $367.93 million, as of February 23, 2008

Yield: 7.47, as of February 23, 2008

COMPANY: GMH COMMUNITIES TRUST

Properties: The company's portfolio is divided into two units: one covers off-campus student housing, and one covers homes for military personnel.

On the student housing side, the company operates more than 95 properties, which consist of about 16,000 units and more than 60,000 beds in college towns such as Chapel Hill, North Carolina, and State College, Pennsylvania. In addition to those properties, the company manages 18 student-housing complexes for other companies, which are made up of 3,000 units and almost 10,000 beds. Going into 2008, the company also owned seven undeveloped or partially undeveloped land parcels it planned on using for student housing.

The company's military personnel homes portfolio covers communities in 21 domestic bases spread over 12 states and Washington, D.C. Some of those projects were in development stages in 2007, but the company projects that when all of its military-based projects are operational, it will have about 17,500 homes in its portfolio.

Details: GMH Associates was initially founded in 1985 with a business model centering on acquiring, developing, and managing commercial and residential real estate, with a focus on student housing.

The company's student housing arm, College Park Communities, models itself as a full-service student home center, with benefits to both the student and the college. From a housing perspective, the company is regularly updating its features to keep pace with a college student's evolving needs. Many of the company's current student housing properties are made up of the following features: private bedrooms, cable television, wired and wireless high-speed Internet access, a washer and dryer in each unit, fitness centers, study areas, and game rooms.

In addition to managing its own portfolio, College Park Communities consults and works with other college student-housing companies,

COMPANY: GMH COMMUNITIES TRUST

providing services such as development, construction management, property management, marketing, leasing, and security.

In 1999, GMH Communities Trust began competing for military housing privatization projects, which involved developing, building, renovating, and managing housing communities for U.S. military personnel and their families.

Much like its student-housing portfolio, the military housing side of the company has been a growth area. The company's involvement in this area stems from the Military Housing Privatization Initiative, which Congress approved in 1996 as part of the National Defense Authorization Act.

Since entering the military housing market, the company has been one of the national leaders in winning contracts, and it said it has been selected for a substantial portion of the projects it has bid on. Its projects stretch through the entire military: the company develops and manages housing projects for at least nine U.S. Army bases, including Walter Reed Army Medical Center; about 20 U.S. Navy bases, in both the Northeast and Southeast; and five U.S. Air Force bases scattered nationwide.

In addition to those core projects, GMH Communities Trust has been chosen by the Army to be its private-sector partner for a renovation project for the family military housing project at West Point.

COMPANY: BERKSHIRE INCOME REALTY

Ticker symbol: BIR.A; shares are traded on the American Stock Exchange

Web site: www.berkshireincomerealty.com

Headquarters: Boston

Founded: 1969; current version of the company went public in 2002.

COMPANY: BERKSHIRE INCOME REALTY

CEO: David Quade (holds title of president and chief financial officer)

Revenues: $73 million in 2006

Market capitalization: $74.51 million, as of February 23, 2008

Yield: .56, as of February 23, 2008

Properties: The company has an ownership interest in 26 apartment communities, including eight in the Baltimore-Washington, D.C. area; four in Virginia; four in Houston; three located in Dallas; two in Chicago; and one each in Charlotte, North Carolina; Atlanta; Tampa; Sherwood, Oregon; and Austin, Texas. The company owns more than 8,000 apartments.

Details: The company's affiliate and predecessor is the Boston-based Berkshire Group, which was founded in 1969 as the Krupp Companies; Douglas Krupp, a well-known Boston-area real estate executive, is the company's board chairman. In addition to its REIT affiliate, the current version of the Berkshire Group is both a real estate investment and financial services firm.

Meanwhile, the current version of the REIT, Berkshire Income Realty, is hyper-focused on apartments in four geographical markets: the Mid-Atlantic, Midwest, Southwest, and Southeastern United States. The company's strategy is to acquire middle-income properties in specific cities it has worked in previously or is otherwise familiar with.

Its avenue of pursuing those properties is Berkshire Advisor, the asset management company it set up to oversee the holdings in its portfolio. This unit develops an annual business plan for each property, factoring in new revenue lines and capital improvement projects. Executives in that unit also monitor expenses, work on new financing strategies, and develop exit plans for selling certain properties.

The parent company has also set up a unit to handle the daily property management and leasing side of its properties, a division its executives say provides the company's biggest revenue growth opportunity.

COMPANY: BERKSHIRE INCOME REALTY

The property division looks for markets with high rent-growth potential by using its industry research and local market experience. The analysis includes researching employment growth numbers, vacancy rates, and competition from other projects in a given market. The research also focuses on growing rental rates by regularly monitoring supply-and-demand forces in its various markets.

One final strategy the company uses is a regular renovation process for each of its properties. First, the company incorporates a physical improvement plan into each property's annual business plan. After that, the individual property managers monitor the apartment complexes to see if any are in need of a major renovation project.

Retail REITs

The last two chapters covered the REITs that focus on the places people work and live: offices and apartments. This chapter will focus on the REITs representing all the shops and stores that sell the stuff that make those offices and apartments function or even thrive.

Known simply as retail REITs, it is a big list in several ways. As of the end of 2007, the National Association of Real Estate Investment Trusts (NAREIT) listed 27 publicly traded equity retail REITs, which were broken down into three sub-categories: shopping centers, of which there were 14; regional malls, of which there were eight; and free standing, for which the association counted five. Taken together, these retail REITs represent the biggest sector among all equity REITs, making up almost 25 percent of the entire portfolio.

The sector is big from a "REIT versus the industry" comparison, too. Apartment and office REITs are in the low-single digits when pitted against the total number of apartment and offices in the country, for example, but the number is much higher for retail REITs. About one-third of regional malls and as much as 50 percent of super regional malls that stretch at least 800,000 square feet are owned and operated by retail REITs. Also, about 15 percent of all non-mall properties, places such as a Wal-Mart- or Home Depot-anchored outdoor shopping plaza, are owned by retail REITs.

The sector is big enough that even the sub-categories have some sub-categories. These include:

- **Neighborhood shopping centers** are anchored by a large regional grocery chain, such as a Publix in the Southeastern United States or a Kroger's in the Midwest. Those stores are in the middle of the complex, in between a variety of smaller stores, from mom-and-pop dry cleaners, to ice cream shops, restaurants, and beauty salons.

   These centers tend to be on the small end of the industry, covering no more than 15 acres. They also tend to be built in bulk, with about one every three to five miles in heavily populated suburban areas.

- **Community shopping centers:** The next step up from neighborhood shopping centers, community shopping centers tend to follow the same concept, only with more size. A community shopping center, for example, might include a regional department store and a national drug store to go along with the grocery store. The centers are bigger, as much as 50 acres, and also come with a bigger geographical reach, covering up to miles of homes.

   The bigger space is often used to add new components, such as gas stations and fast food restaurants to the front of the parking lot. Those properties, known in the industry sometimes as frontage, bring higher rents.

- **Power centers** are designed and planned to be highly visible, in terms of both their location and their anchor tenant. The location tends to be on the outskirts of highly populated suburbs, and more specifically, they are built near major highways to draw from the nearby urban areas, too. The anchor tenant tends to be a big national chain, such as Wal-Mart or Home Depot.

  Power centers also tend to be among the biggest non-mall properties, going as big as 600,000 square feet spread over as many as 100 acres.

- **Outlet malls** are one of the special subsectors of the retail sector, as they speak to the heart of many an American shopper: discounts. Although the malls themselves vary in size nationwide, from as little as 35,000 square feet to as big as 350,000 square feet, the theme of high-end name stores selling merchandise at lower prices remains constant. Most outlet centers have dozens of stores yet do not have one big obvious anchor.

  The biggest and best outlet malls have big geographical reaches, sometimes stretching as much as 75 miles. Some people even make outlet mall shopping a vacation destination.

- **Fashion malls:** This sector is essentially the opposite of outlet malls, as the keys are high-end stores and high-prices, which, short of Christmas or seasonal sales, are not sold at heavy discounts. These malls tend to be smaller in scale, no more than 200,000 square feet, and the anchors are a select group of high-end department stores, such as Nordstrom, Neiman Marcus, and Saks Fifth Avenue.

High-end fashion-style malls tend to be built in high-income areas, such as Long Island, New York, or Southern California.

A Two-Way Street

It should also not come as much of a surprise, given the focus of the past two chapters, that tenants, from the operators of the highest of high-end stores to a shop where every item goes for a buck, go a long way toward making or breaking a retail REIT.

In retail, the tenant-landlord relationship is a two-way street: One side is not likely to reap long-term success without the other side succeeding, too. This is a stark difference from office, apartment, or even hotel REITs, where the REIT operator is relying almost exclusively on outside market forces.

But in retail, regardless of the makeup of the shopping center, if people are not coming through the doors — and buying stuff — then the REIT, as well as the stores therein, could be in trouble. For this reason, retail REIT leases have some special industry-specific features that go past the standard pay per square foot of space.

One common retail REIT lease requirement is officially called a percentage rent. Also known as a breakpoint, this allows the landlord to receive a prenegotiated amount of cash from the retailer if it exceeds a predetermined amount in sales. In return, the landlord has to agree to underwrite certain promotional activities to draw in customers, such as putting up signs, certain advertisements, and hosting promotional events.

The length of a lease in the retail REIT world varies widely, depending on factors such as type of mall or shopping center and the location, not only the part of town the mall is in, but the actual location of the store in the given shopping center. Retail leases tend to be between three to six years — longer than apartments but shorter than offices. This allows flexibility for a landlord looking to move an underperforming tenant out of the complex.

Retail REIT operators — at least the good ones — spend a significant amount of time and effort tracking a retailer's success or failure in terms of sales, since that is so important to the entire complex. This does not mean office or apartment REIT operators ignore the financial well-being of tenants, as that would be counterintuitive.

But take regional mall owners. This segment of retail REITs are hyper-focused on tenant sales, regularly monitoring each store's same-stores growth (stores in operation for a year or more) for every quarter and annually. The REIT operators also factor in sales-per-square-foot numbers for each store.

These measurements provide a gauge for each store's success, as well as the entire mall, when taken together. The numbers also provide a guide for setting future rental rates.

The close first cousin of tenant quality when it comes to retail REITs is the customer base: about 200 million Americans enter some form of a mall, shopping center, or strip plaza every month, numbers that increase significantly during heavy shopping seasons, such as the holidays or back-to-school times.

Key questions include figuring out the demographics and incomes of the shoppers; how often they shop; and, even more important, how often they spend money. For retail REIT operators, two trends that have been percolating over the last ten years are likely to weigh heavily in the game to attract the best customers.

One, quite simply, is the Internet. Retail shopping over the Internet has grown significantly over the last decade, from an estimated $35 billion in 2000 to almost $200 billion in 2007.

Beyond sheer growth numbers, the Internet has clearly been a formidable competitor for traditional brick-and-mortar retailers. Evidence A is the music industry, where before the Internet, national chains such as Tower Records and Best Buy were the kings and queens of selling CDs. The Internet, and more recently, the iPod, has relegated those kings and queens to pawn status. Indeed, as of 2007, Tower Records' United States-based sales were completely Internet driven, as the retailer had closed all of its American stores.

Another trend retail REIT operators are factoring into the cost of doing business is capital expenses, in terms of upgrading mall and shopping center properties. This is integral to being able to recruit and retain top tenants and customers and has only grown costlier the last few years. In the early 1990s, for example, the standard amount retail REIT operators spent on improving properties was about 3 percent to 5 percent of net operating income. That number has been creeping up, to around 8 percent of net operating income by 2007.

As far as returns, the retail REIT sector has been one of the more stable and stellar sectors the last few years. The mostly good times come with a heavy caution flag, though, when looking ahead: in the waning days of 2007 and the early days of 2008, some national economists were predicting that the housing market troubles might mark the beginning of prolonged slump, if not a full-blown recession. If that were to happen, consumer spending would likely take a hit.

In some ways, the hit already came in 2007, as the retail REIT sector spent most of the year down as much as 7 percentage points. This comes on the heels of a robust five-year period from 2002 through 2006, where the sector was up at least 11.8 percent every year, including 46.7 percent in 2003, 40 percent in 2004 and almost 30 percent in 2006, according to NAREIT.

Individual Stories

Here is a glimpse inside four retail REITs with distinct strategies and business models:

COMPANY: SIMON PROPERTY GROUP

Ticker symbol: SPG; shares are traded on the NYSE

Web site: www.simon.com

Headquarters: Indianapolis, Indiana

Founded: 1960; company became Simon Property Group after going public in 1993.

CEO: David Simon

Revenues: $3.332 billion in 2006

Market capitalization: $19.15 billion, as of February 23, 2008

Yield: 4.19, as of February 23, 2008

Properties: The company's portfolio is both international and one of the biggest and most comprehensive of any REIT. In the United States, the company owns outright or holds interest in 320 properties in 39 states and Puerto Rico which are made up of more than 243

COMPANY: SIMON PROPERTY GROUP

million square feet of gross space. Internationally, Simon Property Group has an ownership interest in 52 European shopping centers, including ones in France, Italy, and Poland; five outlet centers in Japan; and one outlet center each in South Korea and Mexico.

Many of the company's properties are well-known shopping destinations. Domestically, the list includes the Forum Shops at Caesars in Las Vegas; the Mall at Chestnut Hill in Boston; Roosevelt Field on Long Island; Sawgrass Mills in Fort Lauderdale, Florida; and the Galleria in Houston. The company also developed and opened the Mall of America in Bloomington, Minnesota, the largest enclosed shopping mall in the country; the property opened in 1992, and Simon sold its interest in it in 2006.

Overseas, the company's star properties include the Arkadia Shopping Center in Warsaw, Poland, and the Gotemba Premium Outlets in Tokyo.

Details: Simon Property Group is one of the largest equity REITs of any kind, in both market capitalization and the total amount of space it controls. It is also the largest publicly traded real estate company in the United States.

It essentially operates five divisions: regional malls, Premium Outlet centers, The Mills Corp., community/life style centers, and international properties.

Developing, managing, and acquiring regional malls was the company's original niche when it was founded in 1960, and it remains well regarded by the retail community in this area.

Simon Property Group's outlet center division portfolio stems from Chelsea Property Group, a publicly traded company Simon bought in 2004. Chelsea, one of the largest outlet center developers and operators in the world, is now run as a Simon subsidiary. The strategy has remained the same under Simon: open high-end outlet centers in or near major metropolitan areas, such as Boston,

COMPANY: SIMON PROPERTY GROUP

Chicago, and New York and in high-traffic tourist markets, such as Las Vegas and Orlando.

The outlet center division is growing, too. It opened two international outlets in 2007, one on South Korea and another one in Japan. In the United States, new outlets are scheduled to open in Houston and on the Jersey Shore in 2008.

The Mills portfolio is Simon Property Group's newest unit. In March 2007, Simon Property Group bought the Mills Corp., which had built up a combination of traditional mall, outlet center, and big-box retailer-anchored shopping centers, totaling 45 million square feet.

Simon Property Group's community/life style division is made up of more than 70 centers comprising 20 million-plus square feet. The properties, which range in size from 30,000 square feet to more than 900,000 square feet, are built in an open-air format and are anchored by a national retailer.

The last component of the company's five-prong strategy is investing in international properties. Simon Property Group made its international investment in 1998, and the division has steadily grown since then. It currently has seven international projects under development, including four in China.

COMPANY: NATIONAL RETAIL PROPERTIES

Ticker symbol: NNN; shares are traded on the NYSE

Web site: www.nnnreit.com

Headquarters: Orlando, Florida

Founded: 1984; current version of the company went public on the NYSE in 1994 and became a self-administered and self-managed REIT in 1998.

CEO: Craig Macnab

Revenues: $149.16 million in 2006

Market capitalization: $1.55 billion, as of February 23, 2008

COMPANY: NATIONAL RETAIL PROPERTIES

Yield: 6.63, as of February 23, 2008

Properties: The company operates more than 900 properties with a cumulative total of more than 10 million square feet, spread across 43 states. Tenants at its shopping centers include Barnes & Noble, Best Buy, CVS, Circle K, and Office Max. As of the end of 2007, the company reported that 98.2 percent of its properties were leased, many of those under triple net lease agreements.

Details: The current version of the company started out as a REIT in 1984, but back then it was called Golden Corral Realty and its shares were traded on the NASDAQ exchange. The company changed its name to Commercial Net Lease Realty, Inc., in 1993, and the next year it began trading on the NYSE.

But the company did not become National Retail Properties until 2006, after a series of other changes, expansions, and acquisitions. Even factoring in all of the changes, one aspect of the company has remained constant: its dividend. The company boasts that it is one of only 181 publicly traded companies out of more than 10,000 that has produced annual dividend increases for 18 consecutive years.

Although the company has several business platforms, its focus has been on triple net leases, which require a tenant to pay a bulk of the costs necessary to keep a property operating at full capacity. These costs include real estate taxes, maintenance, insurance, and utilities. The benefit of a triple net lease structure is that it creates long-term cash flow stability because the tenant pays the spikes in certain costs, such as property taxes.

The company believes in the triple net lease concept so strongly that its stock symbol, NNN, is the real estate industry's moniker for a triple net lease.

In addition to the triple net lease focus, the company concentrates on signing its tenants to long-term leases so that it can protect itself against short-term slowdowns in the retail sector. It has been

COMPANY: NATIONAL RETAIL PROPERTIES

a successful venture. The company's lease terms average 15 to 20 years, and as of late 2007, the company had a 14-year weighted average on its current leases.

National Retail Properties also has several other business lines and revenue streams set up to grow the REIT and its funds from operations (FFO). These include buying and selling properties, build-to-suit developments, joint venture partnerships, and development projects.

The company has also set up a division to facilitate 1031 exchanges, which are also known as Tenant in Common deals. A 1031 exchange allows individual investors to pool their money to buy commercial properties and other large real estate holdings, leaving the management of the actual building to another entity.

COMPANY: TANGER FACTORY OUTLET CENTERS

Ticker symbol: SKT; shares are traded on the NYSE

Web site: www.tangeroutlet.com

Headquarters: Greensboro, North Carolina

Founded: 1981; company went public in 1993

CEO: Stanley K. Tanger (rhymes with hanger)

Revenues: $210.96 million in 2006

Market capitalization: $1.14 billion, as of February 23, 2008

Yield: 3.97, as of February 23, 2008

Properties: The company owns 35 outlet centers totaling about 8.3 million square feet of gross space. Its footprint is diverse, as it owns centers in 23 states, including Alabama, California, Maine, Texas, and Wisconsin. In addition to its own properties, the company also holds a 50 percent ownership stake in two outlet centers totaling 667,000 square feet and manages two other outlet centers totaling 229,000 square feet.

Individual outlet centers tend to be on the outskirts of major

COMPANY: TANGER FACTORY OUTLET CENTERS

population centers. A few, however, are in more unique areas, such as the Tanger Outlet Center in Park City, Utah, which is in the Rocky Mountains, about 6,450 feet above sea level.

Details: Stanley Tanger, who served as a U.S. Air Force pilot in World War II, is considered a pioneer in the outlet mall industry. In 1981, after retiring from running a private label shirt-manufacturing business, Tanger opened a strip center dotted with brand-name factory outlet stores in Burlington, North Carolina.

The outlet center was the first of its kind in the country, bringing together discounts and well-recognized brand names. The concept had grown in popularity in the 1970s, due to a combination of economic factors, such as the energy crisis, which led to consumers having less discretionary income. But no developer had put a diverse collection of stores together in one area until it was done by Tanger.

The outlet concept revolved around price: because consumers were buying directly from the manufacturer, the prices were as much as 40 percent off what it would be in a department store. In the early years, a good portion of outlet center merchandise was damaged or otherwise considered second-tier quality. Merchandise quality has improved as the industry has evolved.

Tanger took the company public in 1993, becoming the first publicly traded company devoted exclusively to outlet mall acquisition, development, and management. The infusion of cash led to a growth spurt for the company, as it opened seven outlet centers over the next two years while also becoming the first outlet center developer to build more than one million square feet of retail space in any one year.

The company continued growing the rest of the 1990s, even attracting the interest of Warren Buffett, who bought a 5.3 percent stake in the company in 1999. By 2007, the company's 35 outlet centers were composed of more than 2,000 stores, with brand-name manufacturers such as Gap, Nike, and Tommy Hilfiger.

COMPANY: CEDAR SHOPPING CENTERS, INC.

Ticker symbol: CDR; shares are traded on the NYSE

Web site: www.cedarshoppingcenters.com

Headquarters: Port Washington, New York.

Founded: 1984; company became Cedar Shopping Centers, Inc. after going public in 2003.

CEO: Leo S. Ullman

Revenues: $126.49 million in 2006

Market capitalization: $508.65 million, as of February 23, 2008

Yield: 7.83, as of February 23, 2008

Properties: The company, which focuses on operating and developing supermarket-anchored community shopping centers and drug-store anchored convenience centers, runs just under 116 properties totaling more than 12 million square feet of gross space. Its geographical focus is in the northeast United States, including a big presence in Pennsylvania, Maryland, and Massachusetts. It also has holdings in Michigan and Ohio.

The company also controls 226 acres of undeveloped land.

Details: The predecessor company to Cedar Shopping Centers, Inc. was Cedar Income Funds, an equity REIT that had been traded on the NASDAQ exchange since 1984 and had a market capitalization of about $13 million at its peak. Industry veteran and real estate attorney Leo Ullman bought Cedar Income Funds in 1998, and in 2003 the company went public on the New York Stock Exchange and changed its name to Cedar Shopping Centers, Inc.

The company breaks down its growth strategy into three areas:

- **Acquisitions:** The company actively seeks to buy stabilized properties that are mostly leased and mostly empty properties, which have solid redevelopment potential. When buying any property, the company tends to gravitate to areas with well-established traffic patterns, strong demographics, and a stable population.

COMPANY: CEDAR SHOPPING CENTERS, INC.

- **Development and redevelopment:** Cedar Shopping Centers has one business unit devoted to planning and implementing "ground-up" development of new supermarket-anchored shopping centers. Another part of the company focuses on renovating, expanding, and changing tenant rosters at existing shopping centers.

- **Property management:** The company had one business division dedicated to managing facilities.

CASE STUDY: KYLE L. MICKALOWSKI

Individual Investor

Location: Sioux Falls, South Dakota

E-mail: klmickalowski@ole.augie.edu

Kyle Mickalowski's young age of 23 proves that REITs are not only for seasoned, experienced investors. Indeed, Mickalowski has been investing in one REIT in particular, Kimco Realty Corp., since he was 19 years old.

Mickalowski says he initially bought shares of the New York City-based retail REIT in January 2004. For the first three years, through February 2007, he says the stock did "very well," more than doubling its share value. The dividend has grown steadily, too, during the time he has owned the stock, to where it was just under 5 percent in the final quarter of 2007.

But from February through the rest of 2007, the stock dropped 33 percent, as did many other REITs during the year.

Mickalowski says his biggest mistake with investing in Kimco is his "lack of understanding in how the macro-economy affects" the stock price. He says he thought that since the company invests

CASE STUDY: KYLE L. MICKALOWSKI

in neighborhood and community shopping centers it would be insulated from the subprime market crisis and credit problems that hit the entire country in 2007. Turns out Kimco's shares dropped anyway, part of a major sell-off of just about every REIT stock in 2007.

Again, defying his age, Mickalowski says he has learned a valuable investing lesson through holding Kimco shares. "High rates of return in REITs are not a sure thing," Mickalowski said. "Investors must understand the effect the macro-economy has on REITs and the key economic signals that affect them."

Mickalowski added an old stand-by that is nonetheless regularly overlooked: a smart investor, Mickalowski says, "should be willing to sell shares as share prices are going up."

Industrial REITs

The industrial REIT sector is marked by both low volatility and, conversely, high predictability. In some ways, potential investors have seen that and thought, "boring."

Indeed, the industrial REIT industry is decidedly non-sexy. These REITs tend to have enormous buildings near ports or self-contained industrial parks. It is nothing like owning a flashy office building downtown, for instance.

Still, unlike office REITs, the cash flow levels in industrial REITs are especially predictable, due mostly to high lease renewal rates and low capital expenses and maintenance requirements. The leases tend be long-term, as long as seven to ten years, do not roll over, and the buildings are so big, that even if a small portion is not under lease, it has little effect on the business operation.

The property behind the investment is, after all, a warehouse. Although there are several types of industrial warehouses that have several uses, one key is simplicity.

There are several stark differences when comparing industrial properties to just about any other type of property a REIT invests in. The structures themselves go up quickly, for example, so there is no need to build one before there is a demand. This prevailing build-to-suit attitude means the sector is normally not too vulnerable to overbuilding.

Also, the industrial sector does not follow the quality-based class grading system used by the apartment and office space industries. Industrial properties are instead broken down by age and how the properties are used, which, although different in principle, is still subjective.

Up until 2007, the one caveat was that the fortunes of the industrial REIT industry had gone up and down based on the economic growth of the United States. If the economy was rolling, like it did in the late 1990s and early 2000s, then, it followed, so to would the industrial REIT industry.

In 2007, though, several REIT executives operating strict industrial portfolios looked outside the United States for properties. This was proving to be a key trend in the sector going into 2008, which, with only six publicly traded industrial-based REITs, according to the National Association of Real Estate Investment Trusts, is still a niche part of the REIT spectrum.

Even with the push to go global, led by big industrial REIT players ProLogis Trust and AMB Property, the concept of what exactly an industrial property is remains somewhat elusive, no matter what country it is in. The tem industrial property is just a generic concept that can be used to define a variety of real estate with functions including production and storage.

The property designations, along with the inherent risk to industrial REIT operators and investors, include:

- **Warehouse:** This is the most common form of industrial property, with close to 7 billion square feet of warehouse space in just the United States alone. Some office buildings have warehouse space, but under the generally accepted marketplace definition, a warehouse must have no more than 10 percent of office space to be considered a warehouse.

Warehouse buildings tend to be somewhat out of the way yet are not far from major transportation areas, be it seaports, railroads, or interstate highways. The buildings also tend to be tall, with ceilings as high as 40 feet. Warehouses are also marked by having multiple loading docks so that trucks can load and unload easily.

Most warehouse leases tend to be industrial-REIT friendly. They often include an annual rent escalation clause due to operating costs, in addition to a clause that puts the onus of paying most of the operating costs on the tenant.

- **Manufacturing:** Pure manufacturing buildings represent a big piece of the industrial property pie, with more than 3 billion square feet nationwide. The actual goings-on inside manufacturing plants differs widely, as the action could be anything from making pens to canning peanut butter.

Manufacturing facilities are further broken down into even smaller subsectors: heavy industrial and light industrial. Heavy industrial manufacturing centers tend be custom-made buildings, good for only that particular tenant. The buildings have reinforced walls and floors, too. Because heavy manufacturing facilities tend to be so specialized, the companies' operating the plants tend to stay in one place and renew leases, rather than spend the money to move equipment somewhere else.

Light industrial facilities tend to be more predicable than their heavy manufacturing counterparts. Light industrial facilities have more stable cash flows, too.

Still, most United States-based manufacturing facilities are owned by the actual company doing the manufacturing, not investors. That is just one barrier for REITs to entering this subsector.

Another barrier, or more to the point, a fear of industrial REIT operators when it comes to investing in manufacturing facilities, is that the sheer nature of making things can be costly and unpredictable.

- **Research and development:** Commonly referred to as flex space, this type of property tends to be smaller than manufacturing and warehouse properties, both in size and scope. Ceilings, for example, tend to be 10 to 15 feet high, and the buildings are sometimes built with showroom windows.

The properties themselves are a combination of office, warehouse, and sometimes even manufacturing space, hence the research and development moniker. The actual amount of each type of space varies widely, depending on the needs of each tenant.

These types of properties are popular with small private companies and industrial REIT operators. Small- to medium-size private companies like the concept because it provides a way to run an entire company under one roof without committing to a big space that might end up being too big. Meanwhile, REIT operators like the space because small to medium-sized businesses make up most of the American business landscape, so there are many opportunities.

The risk for REIT operators investing in research and development facilities is that in many cases these properties, due to the multiple uses, tend to have higher costs.

- **Other:** The rest of the industrial sector has several smaller parts, most of which have been retrofitted for a specific use, such as cold storage or pharmaceutical research. Another type of industrial building, which was more prominent in the late 1990s technology and Internet boom, is what is known as an incubator facility. That is when a landlord takes a bigger property and chops it up into smaller offices to rent the small spaces to startups.

Many times the companies in incubator space are so new and have so little or no revenues, that the rent is paid in the form of company shares given to the incubator's landlord. This certain high risk, with only possible high reward, tends to scare off potential REIT operators.

Going Global

As far as REIT operators are concerned, there are several facets to the sector that hold true regardless of the property. Tenant costs tend to be low, as the need for constant updating and maintenance is not as big as it is with the apartment sector, for instance.

Industrial tenants tend to be a higher quality, too, as the nature of the business tends to eliminate fly-by-night operations that do not think and act long-term.

Another facet that remains the same regardless of property designation, is the "going global" trend. Although this trend has been praised by financial analysts who follow REITs, there are some risks to investing in properties overseas. Going abroad can lead to higher credit risks and a host of tenant issues, from political and social to language and culture differences.

REIT operators and financial analysts say the idea of going outside the United States is not necessarily an indication that the industrial market or even the economy is suffering stateside. Instead, it is more of a follow-the-money situation, or at least a follow-the-company situation.

Industrial REIT clients, from behemoths such as Nike to small-scale shoe manufacturers, have been looking abroad for opportunities for several years, a position only heightened with the 2007 fall of the American dollar. It would follow that industrial REITs would try to capitalize on that by finding space to rent out to these companies.

Denver-based ProLogis has operations in more than 20 countries, including facilities in Asia, Europe, and North America. Meanwhile, San Francisco-based AMB Property Corp. went from being just in the United States and Mexico in 2002 to operating facilities in more than 10 countries by the end of 2007.

The low volatility, high predictability, and global trend

combined to make the industrial REIT sector one of the top performers of the entire REIT industry in 2007. With just six pure industrial REITs, or 5 percent of the entire REIT industry, the sample is small but productive.

For example, industrial REITs, on average, produced a 0.38 percent return in 2007, according to NAREIT. Although not as stellar as the past years, it was a solid in two ways: one, it was one of only three REIT sectors to finish 2007 without a negative, and two, it marked the ninth straight year of positive returns, according to NAREIT. The industrial sector's best years this decade were 2004 (up 34.1 percent), 2003 (up 33.1 percent), and 2000 (up 28.6 percent).

Individual Stories

Here is a glimpse inside four industrial REITs with distinct strategies and business models:

COMPANY: PROLOGIS

Ticker symbol: PLD; shares are traded on the NYSE

Web site: www.prologis.com

Headquarters: Denver

Founded: 1991; company went public in 1994

CEO: Jeffrey H. Schwartz

Revenues: $2.446 billion in 2006

Market capitalization: $14.10 billion, as of February 23, 2008

Yield: 3.78, as of February 23, 2008

Properties: The company operates more than 2,600 distribution facilities in 100-plus markets throughout North America, Europe, and Asia. The facilities cover about 483 million square feet, and

COMPANY: PROLOGIS

the company leases space to some 4,700 clients in 20 countries, including manufacturers, retailers, and transportation companies.

Details: With more than $34.4 billion of real estate under its domain worldwide, ProLogis lays claim to be the largest owner, manager, and developer of distribution facilities in the world. The company, with 1,300 employees across the world, is one of the only REITs of any sector to be both a Fortune 1000 company and included in the S&P 500.

The company was founded in 1991 and initially focused on acquiring properties in the Southwestern United States. By 1993, it expanded to other parts of the country, such as San Francisco, and had 11.4 million square feet of industrial space under management.

In 1994, when the company went public, it had about $400 million in assets under management in nine states. The company went on a growth spurt after the IPO, a stretch that lasted well into the next decade.

The current formation of the company is essentially broken down into three units: property operations, fund management, and a third unit, called CDFS, which develops real estate properties to be sold to other companies.

Property ownership remains ProLogis' niche. In the United States, the company's largest markets are Atlanta, Chicago, Dallas/Fort Worth, New Jersey, and San Francisco. In Europe, the company's biggest presence is in England, and in Asia, its biggest market is in Japan. Most of the properties in Europe and Asia were either bought or developed under the company's CDFS business unit and are pending sale.

For the properties the company is not selling, it continues to earn rent on leases, most long-term deals with reimbursements of some operating costs.

The fund management unit of the company covers long-term investments in property funds. As of 2007, the company managed

COMPANY: PROLOGIS

17 funds valued at $18 billion. In terms of raw properties, the funds own more than 800 properties totaling more than 180 million square feet.

The property fund unit covers two important components for ProLogis: first, it provides an ongoing capital arm, which allows the company to reinvest in other properties. Plus, while managing the properties in the fund, the company collects lease fees and a share of the fund's earnings, which helps diversify the company's revenue stream.

ProLogis also uses its property fund division to maintain relationships with current customers and market and network to find new ones.

The company's CDFS unit mirrors its property operations segment, in terms of being active in North America, Europe, and Asia. The properties under development or in the planning stages in this unit represent buildings already under construction and plots of land.

COMPANY: DCT INDUSTRIAL TRUST

Ticker symbol: DCT; shares are traded on the NYSE

Web site: www.dctindustrial.com

Headquarters: Denver

Founded: 2002

CEO: Phillip L. Hawkins

Revenues: $219.14 million in 2006

Market capitalization: $1.53 billion, as of February 23, 2008

Yield: 7.06, as of February 23, 2008

Properties: As of early 2008, the company's portfolio consisted of 448 properties totaling more than 74 million square feet of space. The properties, which were more than 90 percent occupied as of early 2007, are made up of about 225 bulk distribution facilities, 100 industrial real estate buildings, and 100 light industrial properties.

COMPANY: DCT INDUSTRIAL TRUST

The holdings are spread across 25 high-volume markets in the United States and Mexico, where nearly 800 corporate customers make up the client base.

Details: DCT Industrial Trust's focus on industrial space has allowed it to come up with a coherent strategy that centers on targeting properties for acquisition and development that are near major transportation centers and hubs, close to densely populated markets and have high-quality design standards that allow space to be reconfigured easily.

The company's strategy and business plan also takes a refined, six-pronged approach, including:

- **Capitalizing on acquisition opportunities:** The company plans to grow its portfolio in both its existing markets and in new regions and cities. Specifically, the company is seeking high-quality bulk distribution and light industrial facilities in high-growth markets.

- **Growing its development pipeline:** The company has built up a strong network of relationships with local, regional, and national developers and others in the industry it plans to tap into to create growth. In addition, DCT Industrial executives, according to the company's Web site, also believe that the company's substantial holding of developable land will draw developers from across the country into partnerships.

- **Expanding institutional capital:** Company executives project that the firm's joint ventures, funds, and other commingled investments with institutional partners will have a three-fold effect: the investments, executives predict, will increase the company's return on its invested capital, serve as a supplement to other acquisitions, and increase its access to capital it can use for other growth projects.

DCT Industrial's partnerships in this area are made up mostly of

COMPANY: DCT INDUSTRIAL TRUST

limited liability companies or other joint venture structures, where DCT owns no more than 30 percent of the holdings.

- **Maximizing cash flows:** The company, projecting that there is "embedded rent growth potential" in its properties, according to its Web site, plans on increasing rents and occupancy levels of its existing properties to generate more cash flow.

- **Recycling capital:** The company says it intends to sell non-core assets so it can use the proceeds for new acquisition and development opportunities.

- **Pursuing international growth:** The company plans on adding to its international portfolio, which currently consists of holdings in Mexico. Although DCT hopes to grow internationally outside Mexico, the company is projecting significant growth there, specifically because several of its senior management and directors have Mexico-based commercial project acquisition and development experience.

COMPANY: DUPONT FABROS TECHNOLOGY, INC.

Ticker symbol: DFT; shares are traded on the NYSE

Web site: www.dft.com

Headquarters: Washington, D.C.

Founded: 1997; company went public in 2007

CEO: Hossein Fateh

Revenues: N/A. Company did not disclose revenues before going public.

Market capitalization: $593.85 million, as of February 23, 2008

Yield: 3.58, as of February 23, 2008

Properties: The company currently has five properties up and

COMPANY: DUPONT FABROS TECHNOLOGY, INC.

running, all of which are in Virginia, outside Washington, D.C. The properties, which are wholesale data centers for storing large computer systems, total more than 1 million square feet. The company has several other projects in the works, including ones in California, Illinois, and New Jersey. Current and past clients include Google, Microsoft, and Yahoo!.

Details: Lammot J. du Pont and Hossein Fateh, each of whom had been working in commercial real estate in and around Washington D.C., founded DuPont Fabros Technology in 1997. The partners were seeking a way to capitalize on the explosive growth they were witnessing in the technology sector in the area the mid-1990s.

In addition to commercial real estate, du Pont brought a government and finance background to the firm: he served as a staff member of the U.S. House of Representatives' Committee on Banking & Financial Services from 1993 to 1995.

Fateh and du Pont took the company public October 19, 2007, and despite the uncertain economic times of the debut, the IPO was one of the largest REIT offerings of the year and one of the ten biggest ever among equity REITs. The company raised about $650 million on 30.5 million shares, which closed at $22.55 the first day of trading, just over the forecasted range of $19 to $21 a share.

Now publicly traded, DuPont Fabros Technology is one of the only REITs focusing exclusively on constructing, developing, and maintaining industrial-sized data centers to lease to technology firms. The company's business model revolves around providing long-term, triple net leases to big technology firms seeking to house, power, and cool computer servers and other technology parcels that support the business.

In addition to being long-term, DuPont Fabros Technology says its leases also require reimbursement for property-level operating expenses, have annual rent increases, and with one exception, do not allow early terminations.

COMPANY: DUPONT FABROS TECHNOLOGY, INC.

The trick for the company in return for the lease is in the design and construction of the building, which has to be a combination of high security and high efficiency to pay off for the tenant. From an efficiency standpoint, for example, the company uses systems such as specialized air conditioning that includes using an evaporative chilled water system and rotary backup battery power so that clients can make better use of the space.

Those systems and other features are also based on stable technology and are not tenant-specific, the company says, so they are less likely to become obsolete.

COMPANY: FIRST INDUSTRIAL REALTY TRUST, INC.

Ticker symbol: FR; shares are traded on the NYSE

Web site: www.firstindustrial.com

Headquarters: Chicago

Founded: 1993

CEO: Michael W. Brennan

Revenues: $396.04 million in 2006

Market capitalization: $1.42 billion, as of February 23, 2008

Yield: 9.09, as of February 23, 2008

Properties: The company is in more than 30 markets across the United States, Canada, the Netherlands, and Belgium. Within those markets, it operates more than 400 light industrial properties, 150 research and development/flex properties, 170 bulk warehouses, 100 regional warehouses, and 25 manufacturing properties.

Worldwide, the company has more than 100 million square feet of gross space, with just over 66 million square feet of that space in the United States. Domestically, the company has a heavy concentration of space in large metropolitan areas, such as Dallas/Fort Worth, with 5,735,854 square feet as of September 30, 2007; Minneapolis/St. Paul, with 5,116,369 square feet; and Atlanta, with 4,899,475 square feet.

COMPANY: FIRST INDUSTRIAL REALTY TRUST, INC.

Details: First Industrial Realty Trust is somewhat unique in the industrial REIT sector in that it covers a wide swath of the industrial property terrain, as opposed to just computer server storage or just warehouses. The company has a staff of local real estate executives in each of its to 25 markets who specialize in buying, selling, developing, leasing, and managing the five most prominent industrial categories: light industrial properties, research and development/flex properties, bulk warehouses, regional warehouses, and manufacturing properties.

The company further classifies its light industrial properties as those complexes that total less than 100,000 square feet, have a ceiling height of 16-21 feet and are composed of no more than 50 percent office space or 50 percent of manufacturing space. The company's R&D/flex properties are less than 100,000 square feet, have a ceiling height of less than 16 feet and are composed of 50 percent or more of office space but no more than 25 percent of manufacturing space.

Just like industrial and R&D/flex properties, regional warehouses, under the company's definition, total less than 100,000 square feet of space. The difference is that the ceiling heights in regional warehouses are least 22 feet, and the complexes are made up of no more than 15 percent of office space and no more than 25 percent of manufacturing space.

Bulk warehouses represent the company's biggest properties. The buildings are more than 100,000 square feet, and just like regional warehouses, have a ceiling height of at least 22 feet and are made up of no more than 15 percent of office space and no more than 25 percent of manufacturing space. The final property category, manufacturing, is the most diverse, covering various buildings with a ceiling height of 10 to 18 feet.

In addition to being active in several types of industrial properties, First Industrial Realty Trust has a few more features it says help distinguish itself from other industrial REITs. Included in that list are

COMPANY: FIRST INDUSTRIAL REALTY TRUST, INC.

the company's customer-service initiatives, such as its "two-hour rule," which is a company-wide promise that phone calls placed during normal business hours will be returned within two hours.

The company also says it reviews all of its potential investment opportunities valued at $1 million and up, a low threshold for a company of its size and geographic reach.

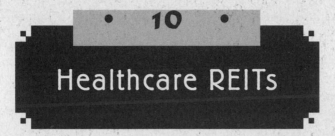

10

Healthcare REITs

The REIT sector devoted to healthcare is one of the most unique, and most complicated, REIT investing options.

That is partly due to the Byzantine structure of the healthcare industry, which, it seems, is on the verge of being overhauled every four years (read: every presidential election). The complications also stem from the structure of the actual investments, which succeed or fail based on access to money from the capital markets.

Although complicated, in some cases, can translate to risky, the risk in healthcare REITs is not any greater than it is in other REITs. Well-managed healthcare REITs that have a sound strategy and a talented staff able to execute it still outperform other investments.

Still, for most of the past 20 years or so, healthcare REITs have been low on REIT investors' wish lists. That has changed since 2006, as equity capital became more accessible and cheaper, and through the end of 2007 there were 11 publicly traded healthcare REITs, according to the National Association of Real

Estate Investment Trusts (NAREIT). That is about 10 percent of the entire industry.

Broken down to its core, healthcare REITs make money through spread investing, which is a method for public companies to manage risk while earning a return rate that exceeds its capital costs. For healthcare REITs, this means finding capital sources and loaning those funds to any number of healthcare providers at higher rates.

The spread comes in the yield, which can trade as many as 500 points over the cost of capital for a well-run and well-managed REIT. A healthcare REIT can then add to the value of each lease by setting it up like a retail lease, where the possibilities for higher earnings are directly tied to the healthcare entity's profits.

The lease rates healthcare REITs can charge are relatively uniform industry wide and are mostly dictated by outside market forces, which means the actual spread, or return, varies little between REITs. That makes the access to capital even more important, as the less a healthcare REIT has to pay to get the money it lends out, the more it can get back.

Access to capital for healthcare REITs works the same for any other company: it comes down to the company's debt rating, which is set by the company's size and market performance.

The other key for healthcare REITs lies in which healthcare business it lends the money to. The list of options is diverse and the potential financial success or failure of these entities is multi-faceted, partially relying on federal government programs such as Medicaid and Medicare.

A healthcare REIT is seeking a financially sound, competent healthcare company that is well located, as far as where competitive properties are, and relatively well maintained. The list of possibilities includes:

Assisted living facilities: These facilities, essentially a dorm for seniors, provide a way for elderly folks to transition from complete independent living to a nursing home with 24-hour care. Residents of assisted living homes tend to have their meals provided and have a list of social and religious activities to choose from.

Assisted living facilities, known as ALFs in healthcare lingo, are also one of the more popular choices for healthcare REIT operators, having grown from about 5 percent of the sector in 2000 to about 35 percent in 2008. This reflects the nationwide growth rate of ALFs, which now includes about 5,000 facilities with more than 500,000 beds.

An average ALF is made up of about 70 beds and is located in high-population pockets and large suburbs. It costs about $5 million to develop and build a typical assisted living facility, making it one of the least expensive options for health companies and entrepreneurs.

Long-term care facilities: Also known as nursing homes or skilled nursing facilities, these operations provide a variety of high-intensity care, mostly to elderly patients with long-term health issues that, while serious, tend to not be serious enough to be treated at an acute care hospital. Specialized nursing home care includes many of the services at congregate care facilities, which combine private rooms with community dining areas

Healthcare REIT operators tend to gravitate toward nursing homes for simple supply-and-demand issues: the supply of nursing home beds nationwide has been severely restricted by state governments seeking to bring down, or at least rein in, Medicaid and Medicare costs. Indeed, most states have set up Certificate of Needs for any nursing home looking to expand, and some states, such as Florida, have established moratoriums on adding any new nursing home beds, save for an emergency.

The limited supply has had the obvious effect of raising the demand for nursing home beds. This demand is expected only to grow over the next few decades, as life expectancies grow and people live longer lives.

Acute care hospitals: A general-service hospital with services including operations, surgeries, radiology, intensive care, labs, rehabilitation therapy, and outpatient care. Stay is less than 30 days. Acute care hospitals make up a little more than 10 percent of the REIT healthcare sector.

Rehabilitation hospitals provide inpatient and outpatient care to people in need of a variety of rehabilitation-based care, such as physical, neurological, speech, and orthopedic therapy. Patients can be either young or elderly, such as stroke victims and those inured an accident.

The sector is both heavily regulated and heavily dependent on federal government reimbursements to make money. That is not a good combination when it comes to potential healthcare REITs, which, save for a few scattered companies, do not tend to invest significantly in rehabilitation hospitals.

Psychiatric facilities provide diagnostic and treatment services for patients under duress or with mental or emotional disorders. This area of healthcare makes up less than 5 percent of the REIT healthcare sector.

Medical office buildings: One of the fastest-growing segments of the healthcare industry, these office buildings house everything from podiatry to pediatrician practices. This category makes up less than 10 percent of the REIT healthcare sector.

Congregate care facilities: From a care perspective, these facilities go one step further than assisted living facilities. Added care includes medication supervision, therapeutic programs and, when necessary, bathing assistance.

Alzheimer's care facilities: Like an alcohol abuse facility, these centers have a singular focus on treating and providing care to those with Alzheimer's disease. Although the concept of an Alzheimer's-only care facility is relatively new to the healthcare spectrum, analysts predict there is little growth in this subsector, due to the high costs.

Alcohol and drug abuse facilities provide counseling and other services to people suffering from alcohol and substance addictions, including detox programs.

Recession Proof

When looking at the myriad of options a healthcare REIT has in investment choices, it is important to point out a significant difference in lease payments between healthcare REITs and

REITs that invest in other properties, including hotels, offices, and warehouses. The difference is that healthcare REITs receive lease payments from one entity, such as a nursing home company operating as many as 50 facilities, while the other REITs tend to receive payments from a host of different tenants.

The importance of the difference is subjective and comes down to risk levels: retail and office REIT operators, for example, will likely say that it is better to have tenant diversity so that if one tenant falters, it is not likely to bring down the entire REIT.

Healthcare REIT operators, however, say that the one-payee system allows them to stay above the fray from problems at one or two facilities in their portfolio. That is, although a retail REIT operator has to be active in making sure all the stores perform well, a healthcare REIT operator has to focus only on making sure the entity's parent company is doing well.

Meanwhile, with the healthcare industry in what seems to be constant upheaval, REITs in this sector have also looked past the actual facilities and medical office parks to generate income. In recent years, some healthcare REITs have sought new property acquisitions, new developments, and even dipped into the mortgage loan side of things.

Expensive investments like those make access to capital markets especially important to healthcare REITs, even more so than when healthcare REITs first started trading publicly in the late 1980s. Back then, the sector was an underground hit with savvy and experienced REIT investors, partially because the investments were as close to as recession proof as possible.

People always have a need for some type of healthcare, from obstetrics to skilled nursing homes.

Despite becoming one of the more volatile REIT sectors, healthcare REITs remain a hit, now because of strong returns and high yields. For example, healthcare REITs are one of the only sectors that had positive compound annual returns from 1997-2007, according to NAREIT. Over that decade, the association reports that healthcare REITs had a ten-year return of 13.38 percent, a five-year return of 20.47 percent, a three-year return of 14.35 percent, and a one-year return of 3.28 percent.

Individually, the sector's best year of the last decade was 2003, when it had a 53.6 percent return.

Individual Stories

Here is a glimpse inside four healthcare REITs with distinct strategies and business models:

COMPANY: HEALTH CARE REIT, INC.

Ticker symbol: HCN; shares are traded on the NYSE

Web site: www.hcreit.com

Headquarters: Toledo, Ohio

Founded: 1970

CEO: George L. Chapman

Revenues: $322.82 million in 2006

Market capitalization: $3.37 billion, as of February 23, 2008

Yield: 6.38, as of February 23, 2008

Properties: The company has 630-plus properties in 38 states, covering a wide range of senior housing and healthcare real

COMPANY: HEALTH CARE REIT, INC.

estate, including skilled nursing homes, hospitals, continuing care retirement communities, long-term acute care hospitals, and medical office buildings. The company runs 234 skilled nursing homes, 201 assisted living homes, and 117 medical office buildings.

From a state perspective, the three states where it has the biggest presence are Florida, where it has 88 properties; Texas, where it has 84 properties; and North Carolina, where it has 53 properties.

Details: Health Care REIT is considered to be the first REIT of any kind to invest exclusively in healthcare properties, which it has been doing in some form since it was founded in 1970.

It is also one of the biggest in the healthcare REIT sector, both in terms of properties it controls and in financial muscle. In 2007, for example, it invested more than $800 million into new projects and developments and expanded its unsecured credit line to $1.15 billion. This was on top of a busy 2006, when the company completed gross and net investments of $559.2 million and $418 million, respectively, while investing another $158.6 million in new projects and identifying $2 billion to $3 billion worth of future opportunities.

In 2006, the company bought Windrose Medical Properties Trust for $1 billion. After the deal, Healthcare REIT chief executive George Chapman said the deal enabled the company to reach a critical mass in several healthcare and senior housing sectors that would have otherwise taken as long as five years to reach. The Windrose purchase also accomplished other goals for Health Care REIT: first, the combined company had a more diversified list of properties, which lowered the risk of the company, and second, the company took on several properties that were not as dependent on governmental revenues.

Including the Windrose properties and assets, the current makeup of Health Care REIT is broken up into two parts, one for property management and one for development services.

The company's real estate group is a Palm Beach Gardens, Florida-

COMPANY: HEALTH CARE REIT, INC.

based subsidiary called Paramount Real Estate Services. Paramount, founded in 1998, handles the company's property management, leasing, and brokerage service, focusing on hospitals and medical office buildings and complexes.

Meanwhile, Health Care REIT's development services group, which was formerly known as Hospital Affiliates Development Corp., provides planning, design, development, finance, and management services to healthcare systems and physician groups. The company has consulted on more than 600 projects, stretching across 35 states and 15 countries, worth more than $1.8 billion.

COMPANY: VENTAS

Ticker symbol: VTR; shares are traded on the NYSE

Web site: www.ventasreit.com

Headquarters: Louisville, Kentucky

Founded: 1999; company operated as non-REIT healthcare firm before 1999.

CEO: Debra A. Cafaro

Revenues: $415.85 million in 2006

Market capitalization: $5.74 billion, as of February 23, 2008

Yield: 4.77, as of February 23, 2008

Properties: The company's portfolio consists of more than 500 healthcare facilities scattered across 43 states and two Canadian provinces. As of early 2007, the holdings were broken down into about 250 senior housing properties, 200 skilled nursing home facilities, 40 hospitals, and multiple office complexes.

Details: With the exception of its medical office buildings, the company leases its properties through triple net, pooled, multi-facility leases, sometimes referred to as master leases. The triple net lease requires a tenant to pay a bulk of the costs necessary to keep a property operating at full capacity. These costs can include real estate taxes, maintenance, insurance, and utilities.

COMPANY: VENTAS

The triple net lease structure has provided the company a method of achieving long-term cash flow stability, which, in turn, has led to strong funds from operations (FFO) growth. In 2007, for instance, the company reported that its normalized FFO per share increased by 10 percent, one of the highest growth rates in the industry. The end of 2007 was also the sixth consecutive year the company reported double-digit normalized FFO per share growth.

The company's net lease structures, along with some other strategy points, have also led to strong results in other financial reporting areas.

For example, the company has been one of the top-performing healthcare REITs from 2002-2007 in terms of shareholder returns. Results over that time period include a 12 percent annual return for 2007; a 23.9 percent return for the three-year period ending December 31, 2007; and a 38.6 annual return for the five-year period ending December 31, 2007. The company performed well over the past decade, too, posting a 19.1 percent compound annual return for the ten-year period ending December 31, 2007.

Outside of simply seeking triple net and other high-return leases, the company maintains a core strategy of monitoring and analyzing the changes happening to the country's aging population. It does this through its roughly 250 senior housing facilities, which provide housing to the nation's growing segment of seniors who live in a community setting and require limited or no medical care.

Another segment of the healthcare market that Ventas focuses on is skilled nursing homes, which provide care to the country's growing segment of seniors that have long-term healthcare needs. With 200 skilled nursing homes nationwide in its portfolio, the company looks to leverage its status as one of the leaders in this industry subsector.

That plan gets an external boost, as the skilled nursing home facility

COMPANY: VENTAS

segment is considered a "high barrier to entry" part of the healthcare spectrum for a variety of reasons, including state regulatory hurdles, long construction lead times, and low medical reimbursements.

One final component of the company's long-range business strategy is its geographic diversity. On a percentage basis, for instance, only two states account for more than ten percent of the company's revenues. The company's 44-state portfolio helps it mitigate risks, both in the economy and in healthcare specific situations, such as state regulations and medical reimbursements.

COMPANY: HCP, INC.

Ticker symbol: HCP; shares are traded on the NYSE

Web site: www.hcpi.com

Headquarters: Long Beach, California

Founded: 1985

CEO: James F. Flaherty

Revenues: $534.89 million in 2006

Market capitalization: $6.38 billion, as of February 23, 2008

Yield: 6.20, as of February 23, 2008

Properties: The company holds an ownership stake in 753 properties spread across 43 states, focusing on the senior housing, medical office, life science, hospital, and skilled nursing sectors; it also has some holdings in Mexico.

As of September 30, 2007, HCP's real estate portfolio was worth $11 billion, and it had a development pipeline of other projects worth more than $2 billion.

Details: The company was officially named Healthcare Property Investors, Inc. until it changed its name to HCP in July 2007. The new name, the company said, did a better job recognizing the evolution of the business.

COMPANY: HCP, INC.

When the company was founded in 1985, its portfolio consisted of two acute care hospitals and 22 skilled nursing facilities. It has since grown to its current levels through a combination of its own development projects and by buying other companies, such the 2007 acquisition of Slough Estates USA, Inc. HCP paid $2.9 billion for Slough Estates, a United Kingdom-based commercial real estate firm that operates 83 properties in the life sciences industry, totaling more than 5.2 million square feet of space.

The Slough Estates deal only further solidified what HCP has long said is a key strategy for the company: diversification. The company claims to have the largest and most diversified portfolio of any healthcare REIT, and it says that holding such a large variety of locations, industries, and individual companies enables it to mitigate long-term risk. Diversification also enables the company's management team to look into a wider range of potential new business opportunities, as opposed to focusing on a specific industry or property type.

Diversification is one of three components of what the company calls its business strategy triangle. The second leg is its conservative balance sheet, which the company says provides the financial resources that allow it to respond quickly to those new business opportunities. In addition to direct investment in healthcare properties, the company's total portfolio and balance sheet include joint ventures, other partnerships, and mortgage/mezzanine loans. The third leg of HCP's strategy triangle is what it called opportunistic investing. The company says it is constantly seeking the best real estate deals to help reach its goal of "driving profitable growth." In 2006, a year before the Slough Estates acquisition, the company closed on another deal it considered opportunistic. This one was a $5.3 billion deal for CNL Retirement Properties, Inc., which, at the time of the deal, was the third largest healthcare REIT in the country.

CNL Retirement Properties, founded in Orlando in 1998, had built up

COMPANY: HCP, INC.

a portfolio around independent living, assisted living, and continuing care retirement communities, along with holding some medical office buildings and other medical real estate. Commenting at the time of the deal, HCP executives said the CNL acquisition was a quick and economical way to add more than 250 properties to the company's portfolio while also opening doors for new owner/operator relationships. CNL's clients included some of the most well known in the senior housing industry, such as Sunrise Senior Living, Horizon Bay, and Erickson Retirement Communities.

COMPANY: UNIVERSAL HEALTH REALTY INCOME TRUST

Ticker symbol: UHT; shares are traded on the NYSE

Web site: www.uhrit.com

Headquarters: King of Prussia, Pennsylvania

Founded: 1986

CEO: Alan B. Miller

Revenues: $32.51 million in 2006

Market capitalization: $399.32 million, as of February 23, 2008

Yield: 6.88, as of February 23, 2008

Properties: The company operates more than 45 investments spread across 14 states, with a property portfolio that includes 35 medical office buildings, six acute care hospitals, four preschool and child care centers, one rehabilitation hospital, one behavioral healthcare facility and one sub-acute care facility.

The largest facility in its portfolio is McAllen Medical Center in McAllen, Texas. The company also has facilities in Arizona, Georgia, and Kentucky.

Details: Universal Health Realty Income Trust, founded by hospital and real estate veteran Alan Miller in 1986, has a significant connection to another company Miller founded: Universal Health Services. The latter company, which is not a REIT, was founded in 1978 and has since grown to become a 38,000-employee hospital and healthcare

COMPANY: UNIVERSAL HEALTH REALTY INCOME TRUST

property management company with $4.19 billion in 2006 revenues. Miller serves as chairman and president of both companies.

The connection between the companies is deeper than just sharing a top executive. Universal Health Services is the REIT's principal tenant, accounting for 49 percent of the trust's revenues in 2006. Also, going into 2007, Universal Health Services' subsidiaries were leasing four of the six hospital facilities owned by Universal Health Realty Income Trust, with some of the leases not scheduled to expire until 2011 and in some cases not until 2014. Another connection is through UHS of Delaware Inc., a UHS healthcare consulting firm that serves as the REIT's chief investment adviser.

Aside from its connections to Universal Health Services, the REIT makes more than half of its revenues from the hospital business. Indeed, investments in hospital facilities accounted for 56 percent of Universal Health Realty Income Trust's net revenues in 2006.

Although the company had some financial success in 2006, parts of 2007 were more difficult, especially in the area of net income. For example, over the first nine months of 2007, it reported $18.21 million, or $1.53 a share, in net income, a significant drop from the $27.57 million, or $2.32 a share it reported in the first nine months of 2006. The company's third quarter net income drop was even more acute: it went from $15.73 million, or $1.32 a share, in the 2006 third quarter to $4.43 million, or $0.37 a share, for the same time in 2007.

The good news is that reason for the drop, the company said, was not a long-term or ongoing event. The company put the onus for the fall in net income on replacement costs at one of its properties, Chalmette Medical Center in Louisiana. The REIT reported that it received a $20,000 gain in replacement costs in the 2007 third quarter from Chalmette, a paltry sum compared to the $11.3 million it received from the hospital in the 2006 third quarter, which it said explained the net income disparity.

11

Self-Storage REITs

With only four publicly traded self-storage REITs at the end of 2007, the self-storage category is the smallest equity REIT sector. Because self-storage facilities tend to be boxy, non-descript buildings with a simplified business plan, the sector is also one of the more boring ones on the market. Indeed, it ranks up there with the industrial REIT sector in boredom levels.

Still, boring and small does not mean the self-storage REIT sector is lacking opportunities.

The self-storage industry came to fruition in the southwestern United States in the 1940s and 1950s as a way for transient military personnel to store belongings. At first, many people in the industry, even the ones operating the actual facilities, thought of self-storage as a temporary use of land until something better came along.

The industry grew along with America's stuff-accumulation boom of the 1970s and 1980s. The fact that millions of people were moving to California and Florida, where most homes are built without basements, only added to the appeal of self-storage facilities.

Then, in the early 1980s, the industry had an epiphany-like moment: self-storage operators realized they did not have to insure the goods, much like competing moving companies did when storing goods. Without having to pass on an insurance cost to customers, an entire new pricing structure was born.

The industry took off. By the mid-1980s, there was just under 300 million square feet of self-storage space. But by 2007, there was 2.2 billion rentable square feet of self-storage space. The industry is now made up of more than 51,000 self-storage facilities, with a cumulative value of $22.6 billion, according to the Self Storage Association, an industry trade group.

Individual use of self-storage facilities has grown steadily, too, from about one in 17 households in the mid-1990s to one in ten in 2007.

REITs make up a tiny, albeit growing, part of the fragmented self-storage landscape. About 40 percent of all the self-storage facilities in the country are owned by entrepreneurs who own just the one facility, according to the association, while another 45 percent or so are run by small businesses that have a portfolio of about 10 to 15 facilities.

That leaves about 3,000 self-storage facilities that are run by REITs. Although those REITs are four of the biggest self-storage operators in the country, combined, the trusts make up less than 5 percent of the entire industry.

The market share might be small, but there are several ways a REIT-operated self-storage facility can stand out. In addition to simply having more access to capital, a self-storage REIT can also separate itself from mom-and-pop self-storage facilities in the following ways:

- **Branding and marketing:** This is one of the few real estate sectors where a brand name and marketing program can matter. In comparison to an office complex or an apartment community, a self-storage company can market itself on a national basis.

- **National diversification:** An entrepreneur that operates only one self-storage facility is completely reliant on that facility to prosper. But a self-storage company with a national presence will have an easier time absorbing underperforming markets. A portfolio of facilities in various geographic areas also provides a more stable cash flow, which in turn can reduce capital costs.

  The cash flow produced by self-storage REITs is also diverse, coming from multiple facilities, which have even more multiple tenants.

- **Other products:** The reach of the bigger self-storage providers also provides an avenue to sell other, high-margin products, such as truck and van rentals and packing materials and boxes.

- **Customer service:** The same reach can be used to provide better customer service, such as operating a call center where potential clients can call from any location with questions about a certain property. Out-of-town customers feel more comfortable leasing space this way.

Self-storage facilities have several other perks a REIT operator can use when pursuing solid returns. First, the structures themselves tend to be easy and relatively inexpensive to build. The construction process is repetitive and simplified, and materials tend to cost less.

Second, the margins tend to be high, mostly because expenses tend to be low. Management costs are minimal, as even a large self-storage facility requires only a two- or three-person management staff. Heating and cooling costs are lower than most other types of properties, such as retail stores, offices, and apartments, as there is less space to heat up or cool down. Because the structures are just garage-sized rooms, maintenance and upkeep costs are kept low.

A third positive attribute of self-storage REITs is seen through its lease structure. Because the industry has monthly leases, it can raise rents more quickly due to market forces than just about any other commercial real estate segment. Of course, the flip side is true with this too: if the supply-and-demand market forces are on the side of the consumer, a self-storage operator might have to lower rates just as quickly to stay competitive.

As with any other REIT sector, there are other risks involved in operating self-storage REITs. Just like the lease structures, the risks tend to be the opposite of the advantages.

For instance, the low construction costs could turn out to be a negative because they could lead to an overbuilding situation. Cheap construction costs can also translate to lowering the barrier to entering the market, which would heighten competition, another potentially negative situation.

A Growing Industry

The key to the industry, according to Wall Street analysts and REIT operators, is figuring out the whos and wheres of the customer base. Because one recent industry trend in 2006-2007 as been going global, this facet of the industry only promises to get more challenging.

Individually, customers in the self-storage industry make up a diverse lot. The list includes military personnel, which remain an industry staple; college students in need of summer storage; and empty nesters and retirees downsizing their living arrangements. Other customers include people going through divorces, family deaths, and job transfers.

The other side of the self-storage customer base is other businesses. The commercial category represents anywhere from 25 percent to 33 percent of the entire self-storage customer base.

The combination of individual and commercial clients helps self-storage operators spread their revenue stream around, which mitigates risk.

The locations of self-storage facilities have evolved along with the industry and the customer base. The days of building the facilities in out-of-the-way industrial areas are about over. Self-storage operators now go the car-wash route: look for busy intersections in high-traffic areas near places where people have lots of stuff, such as large housing subdivisions and apartment complexes.

Another trend has been to incorporate self-storage facilities as part of a mixed-use development that includes retail space. For example, Simon Property Group, the retail REIT known for its shopping malls, recently announced its plans to work some self-storage facilities into some retail developments.

There is the trend of going to Europe, following a recent development in the industrial REIT sector. The European industry is about one-tenth the size of the United States market, analysts say, and Europeans are just beginning to catch on to the concept. The United States-based company with the biggest presence overseas is Public Storage, which is also the largest self-storage REIT.

The upshot of the industry, after factoring in the type of customer and the location of the facility, is one of growth. The self-storage REIT sector has grown steadily, too, at least until 2007, when it was hit by the nationwide housing slowdown. In 2007, the sector was down 4.51 percent, according to the National Association of Real Estate Investment Trusts (NAREIT).

The sector's long-term results, though, are much better. According to NAREIT, through 2007, the sector produced a three-year return of 13.69 percent, a five-year return of 21.26 percent, and a ten-year return of 14.17 percent. Individually, the sector's best years of the past decade were 2001, when it produced a 43.2 percent return, and 2003, when it produced a 38.1 percent return.

Individual Stories

Here is a glimpse inside four self-storage REITs with distinct strategies and business models:

COMPANY: PUBLIC STORAGE

Ticker symbol: PSA; shares are traded on the NYSE

Web site: www.publicstorage.com

Headquarters: Glendale, California

Founded: 1972

CEO: Ronald L. Havner Jr.

Revenues: $1.381 billion in 2006

Market capitalization: $13.80 billion, as of February 23, 2008

Yield: 2.60, as of February 23, 2008

Properties: The company operates more than 2,100 self-storage facilities totaling 135 million rentable square feet. Its units are spread across 38 states in the United States and seven countries in Western Europe.

In addition to its individual self-storage units, Public Storage has an equity interest in PS Business Parks, an affiliate that operates 19 million square feet of commercial and industrial storage space across eight states.

Details: Public Storage, which is a member of the S&P 500 and the Forbes Global 2000, is by far the largest of the four publicly traded self-storage REITs. It only got bigger in 2006, when it bought Shurgard Storage Centers, Inc., the second biggest self-storage REIT.

The Shurgard deal only heightened what has long been a Public Storage focus: operating the business with a strong infrastructure, both in employees and actual self-storage facilities. The infrastructure includes comprehensive national advertising and marketing campaigns, which revolve around the company's well-known orange and blue logo and color scheme.

From a public markets perspective, the company has been a Wall Street favorite for a few years, as its funds from operations (FFO) have not suffered significantly from the mergers and acquisitions, such as the big one with Shurgard. Also, the company regularly beat Wall Street revenue projections in 2007, even as the industry

COMPANY: PUBLIC STORAGE

felt some pressure from the national housing slump.

Public Storage's success, especially in 2007, could turn into its biggest challenge in the next few years. In its 2007 third quarter earnings release, for example, the company attributed a $71 million net revenue increase partly to a $30 million-plus gain in foreign currency exchange, courtesy of its European units combining with the weak American dollar.

Although that looks good on paper for short-term purposes, the European side of the business, which it acquired in the Shurgard deal, was in jeopardy. As of early 2008, the company, according to some published reports and Wall Street analysts, had dropped plans to spin the European unit off into own public offering and instead was seeking to sell a majority stake in the operation.

If and when the company sells of some of its European holdings, the challenge then becomes how to grow the American side of the business during a housing slump that put many regions of the United States on recession watch in 2007. Although the company used its size and high-efficiency operating features to avoid being brought down by the housing market in 2007, that could change as the slump grows longer and bigger: fewer people buying houses means fewer people moving, which in turn could mean fewer people seeking storage space.

COMPANY: SOVRAN SELF STORAGE

Ticker symbol: SSS; shares are traded on the NYSE

Web site: www.unclebobs.com

Headquarters: Williamsville, New York

Founded: 1982

CEO: Robert J. Attea

Revenues: $166.29 million in 2006

Market capitalization: $802.25 million, as of February 23, 2008

Yield: 6.81, as of February 23, 2008

COMPANY: SOVRAN SELF STORAGE

Properties: The company, operating under the trade name Uncle Bob's Self Storage, owns and/or operates more than 350 self-storage facilities spread across 22 states, totaling more than 20 million rentable square feet. Its properties and facilities, which range between 22,000 square feet and 188,000 square feet, serve about 140,000 tenants.

Its locations mirror population-growth patterns, as its biggest presence is in Texas, where it has 77 facilities; Florida, where it has 52 facilities; and Georgia, where it has 26 facilities. With the exception of Texas and Arizona, all of the company's other facilities are in states east of the Mississippi River, including Alabama, Michigan, and New Hampshire.

Details: The core strategy at Sovran Self Storage is based on two concepts: seeking other self-storage facilities it can buy to grow and developing and using new products and initiatives it says can help make the company more efficient.

From a growth perspective, the company, which has about 1,000 employees spread over its various locations, has several benchmarks in marketing, maintenance, and finances that have to be met when looking at any potential acquisition.

The list includes properties that fit the company's self-storage facility template. That means having well-lit facilities secured by gates that have computerized entry. It also means single-story properties, which allow all customers to have direct vehicle access to their storage unit.

Next, the company seeks only single facilities in markets it is already in, as compared to looking for multiple facilities in what would be a new market.

Over the past two years, Sovran has made several acquisitions that met those requirements. In March 2007, for example, the company announced that it had bought 12 self-storage facilities from three

COMPANY: SOVRAN SELF STORAGE

different companies for a total of $44 million. Included in the purchase list were 9 facilities in Western New York, which is also where the Sovran company headquarters is located. At the time of the deal, which bumped the company's Western New York store count to 15, Sovran chief executive Robert J. Attea said the acquisition quickly accomplished a long-term goal of expanding its retail presence in the company's hometown.

A few months after those deals, the company announced it had bought 14 more facilities, in a combination of new and existing markets. Stores it bought in existing markets included a pair in Pensacola, Florida, and another two facilities in Montgomery, Alabama. New markets it entered through the deal include Huntsville and Mobile, Alabama.

Whether the acquisitions represent new or old markets, the company tries to make use of new products a priority at every facility, to increase and diversify its revenue stream. One of those products, which it has implemented in many of its units, is Dri-guard, a state-of-the-art dehumidification system it uses to control the air quality and temperature readings.

Sovran also operates a national customer service center, which uses a fully integrated sales and reservation system. Some Sovran customers even pay their bills over the Internet, which is not as common in the self-storage industry as it is in other industries.

COMPANY: U-STORE-IT TRUST

Ticker symbol: YSI; shares are traded on the NYSE

Web site: www.u-store-it.com

Headquarters: Cleveland

Founded: 1970; company went public in 2004

CEO: Dean Jernigan

Revenues: $213.11 million in 2006

Market capitalization: $527.96 million, as of February 23, 2008

COMPANY: U-STORE-IT TRUST

Yield: 7.87, as of February 23, 2008

Properties: The company owns about 410 self-storage facilities in 27 states, totaling more than 26 million rentable square feet. Going into 2007, about 80 percent of the company's units were under lease contracts, representing about 173,000 tenants.

The facilities, of which just over half are climate-controlled units, are in a geographically diverse lot of states, including California, Colorado, Indiana, New York, New Mexico, Ohio, and Tennessee. Its top markets are Florida, representing about 18 percent of its total portfolio; California, representing about 13 percent of its portfolio; and Ohio, representing about 8 percent of the portfolio.

Details: Officially, U-Store-It Trust executives say their strategy is to grow the company's portfolio by being on the buying side of the consolidation period the industry has been going through the past few years. The company says its acquisitions are designed to increase its economy of scale, by spreading its "management expertise and operating efficiency across a larger portfolio." The company hopes that effort, in turn, will increase its cash flow through charging higher rents, reaching higher occupancy, and bringing down operating expenses.

The company has essentially been following that strategy since its October 2004 IPO. Back then, it had just over 200 properties. In July 2005, the company bought National Self-Storage, giving it more than 300 facilities in 25 states. More purchases followed through late 2007, bringing the company to the 400-plus self-storage facilities it currently owns.

Although the company continues its effort to execute its growth strategy, it was distracted for most and 2007 and parts of 2006 by a legal battle pitting Robert Amsdell, the company's cofounder, former chairman, and chief executive and some of his family against U-Store-It Trust's current management team.

COMPANY: U-STORE-IT TRUST

At one point, both U-Store-It had sued Amsdell and the Amsdell side had sued U-Store-It.

First, the company said Robert Amsdell, along with his son Todd Amsdell, president of a company subsidiary, violated their contracts and conspired against the company to benefit their own firm, Rising Tide Development. The company alleged that the Amsdells manipulated occupancy rates at some of their Rising Tide self-storage facilities to trigger a buying clause, putting U-Store-It on the hook to buy the entities.

Meanwhile, in addition to denying the accusations, both Robert and Todd Amsdell responded by filing countersuits, according to published reports of the disputes. In one suit, Robert Amsdell accused the company's chief executive officer, Dean Jernigan, of trying to take company power away from the Amsdell family, according to those reports.

The legal battles ended September 14, 2007. That is when U-Store-It Trust announced it had bought 14 self-storage facilities that were operated by the Amsdell family's Rising Tide Development for $121 million. In addition to the acquisition, the company said all of the legal disputes had been settled.

COMPANY: EXTRA SPACE STORAGE INC.

Ticker symbol: EXR; shares are traded on the NYSE

Web site: www.extraspace.com

Headquarters: Salt Lake City, Utah

Founded: 1977; company went public in 2004

CEO: Kenneth M. Wooley

Revenues: $197.26 million in 2006

Market capitalization: $980.14 million, as of February 23, 2008

Yield: 6.66, as of February 23, 2008

Properties: The company has a portfolio of more than 600 self-storage facilities spread across 32 states and Washington, D.C. The facilities,

COMPANY: EXTRA SPACE STORAGE INC.

which total more than 400,000 individual storage units composed of about 45 million square feet of net rentable space, are broken down into about 340 facilities that the company owns in joint venture partnerships and another 260 that it owns outright. The company also operates about 75 other self-storage properties that are owned by franchisees or other third parties.

Details: The company essentially operates in two segments. One is property management and development, where it concentrates on maintaining and improving its current facilities, in addition to looking for new acquisition opportunities. The other segment the company focuses on is in rental operations, which is the day-to-day management side of the business.

In both segments, the company has been on a massive growth spurt since its 2004 initial pubic offering, to the point where as of early 2008, it was one of the three largest self-storage firms in the country. The growth has been spurred mostly by acquisitions.

Some deals were of the small-scale variety, mostly to foster expansion plans in geographic markets the company had not yet entered. But one deal in particular significantly altered both the company and the self-storage industry. That happened in 2005, when Extra Space Storage bought one-time competitor Storage USA and its 416 properties for $2.3 billion.

The deal, a joint venture with Prudential Real Estate Investors, nearly tripled the size of Extra Space Storage, in terms of facilities under company ownership. It was also the biggest transaction ever in the self-storage industry.

Even though the Storage USA deal ultimately gave Extra Space Storage a presence in 32 states, the company's revenue stream and growth stem mostly from its facilities on the West and East Coasts. Indeed, about 80 percent of its properties are located in coastal states and cities, including California, Florida, Boston, New York, and Washington, D.C.

COMPANY: EXTRA SPACE STORAGE INC.

As of 2006, the company was still embarking on its growth strategy, putting about $180 million toward developing new properties. Many of those were planned for coastal markets too, where company executives say the projects have better long-term appreciation.

In addition to growing its presence and market share, Extra Space Storage is also looking to improve on some of its core business principles. Those include maximizing customer satisfaction, creating a top-tier working environment for its nearly 2,000 employees, and developing more mutually beneficial partnerships and joint ventures.

CASE STUDY: ANATOLE PEVNEV

Westlake, Ohio

www.reitcafe.com

When longtime REIT research analyst Anatole Pevnev bought his teenage daughter an iPod a few years ago, he thought of the MP3 player as a nice innovation of a music gadget.

But he did not think of it then as an avenue to disseminate REIT information, data and news. Pevnev spotted an opportunity in October 2005, though, as podcasts with all kinds of content, from sports highlights to talk radio shows, began gaining popularity.

"It occurred to me that this was a good way to get information out to investors that they normally would not have," said Pevnev, a former REIT analyst with research firms McDonald Investments and Legg Mason.

Thus, REITcafe was born. Since debuting in late 2005, the Web site, **www.reitcafe.com**, has become a clearinghouse of REIT information including constantly updating news postings, blogs, and correlation charts, with a running commentary. The site, under

CASE STUDY: ANATOLE PEVNEV

Pevnev's direction, has even created a REIT volatility index, to monitor the volatility levels of the industry.

But REITcafe's most popular feature, in the view of many individual investors and institutional research analysts, is the podcast section. This is where Pevnev, calling on his years of industry experience and contacts, interviews a variety of REIT executives. For example, a recent posting included an interview with Feldman Mall Properties chairman Larry Feldman, where, among other questions, Pevnev asked about the company's delayed financial reports and its decision to "explore strategic alternatives."

As of early 2008, the site had posted 140 interviews with executives, analysts, and other key figures in the industry. In addition to the interviews, the site posts industry conference calls hosted by the National Association of Real Estate Investment Trusts (NAREIT) and individual companies. All of the information on the Web site, including the podcasts, is free.

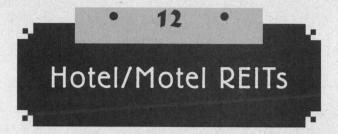

Hotel/Motel REITs

Hotel REITs are known first and foremost for their volatility, a factor that stems directly from the sector's economic sensitivity. Because hotel and motel rooms are a daily, weekly, or sometimes monthly business transaction, there are no long-term leases to stretch out cash flow. Therefore, the business is dependent on constant turnover.

The sector's dependence on economic cycles has spawned another challenge for the industry, that of management. A well-managed hotel or chain of hotels can withstand economic downturns better than lesser-managed hotels by relying on branding and reputation. Managers, both individual and from a corporate perspective, can do a lot to improve a hotel's standing in the marketplace. This includes adjusting rates higher or lower to stay competitive, as well as adding amenities, such as room service, a pool, or other recreational activities, to enhance the guest experience.

This is how chains such as Hilton and Marriott have grown into successful worldwide brands.

The management challenge has an advantage over the economic

challenges in that running a hotel business, for better or for worse, is something a REIT operator has direct control over. Economic cycles, such as the tourism industry slump caused by the September 11 terrorist attacks, are essentially out of a REIT operator's control.

In the middle of those challenges lies the sector's greatest Achilles' heel: overbuilding. In the late 1980s and the early 1990s, for example, the industry went on a building tear that ultimately pushed down prices, as supply peaked. The construction slowed by the mid-1990s, which led to both a boom in the industry and in hotel REITs. Indeed, in a three-year period ending in 1996, ten hotel REITs launched public offerings worth more than $1 billion cumulatively.

The cycle continued spinning, though, with overbuilding taking center stage again in late 1990s. Combined with the post-September 11, 2001, slowdown, that overbuilding phase was not absorbed until 2004 and 2005, industry experts say.

The early days of the hotel industry were significantly simpler. There were fewer brands and fewer types of hotels. Of course, that simplicity translated to fewer choices, and it follows, fewer travelers and lower revenues and profit margins.

For a time, the hotel/motel industry, otherwise known as lodging, consisted of two categories: destination facilities and transient facilities. Destination hotels, by definition, are ones that are seeking guests on vacation, business, or some combination of the two, such as a convention. Destination hotels are often located in resort cities or places popular with tourists, such as Orlando and Las Vegas.

Transient facilities, meanwhile, are hotels and motels located near transportation hubs, such as airports and interstate highway interchanges. Many transient-type properties tend offer lower-priced rooms than destination hotels, but not all transient hotel properties are low-budget, no-frills operations. A significant number of roadside and airport hotels have spent considerable time and money on improvement projects, adding features such as free in-room Internet connections.

The growth of the industry has led to more specific categories of hotels and motels. These include:

Luxury hotels: There are a limited number of players in this category, as the judging parameters are, by nature, tough to achieve. On a national scale, chains such as the Four Seasons, the Waldorf Astoria, and the Ritz-Carlton qualify as four- and five-star luxury hotels. Other luxury hotels are independent and boutique operations, found in medium-sized cities.

Business hotels cater to the business traveler but also have a piece of so-called affordable luxury in an effort to attract high-end leisure travelers. The facilities tend to be located in mid-size and large cities and come equipped with meeting room space and a restaurant and lounge/bar area. The room rates are considerably lower than luxury hotels.

Hotel chains that have business hotels include Crown Plaza, Hilton, Hyatt, Marriott, Sheraton, and Westin.

Mid-market hotels may be the largest category of hotel segments. It includes the standard, full-service model, such as Hampton Inn, Holiday Inn, and Howard Johnson — facilities that have restaurants and meeting rooms but tend to be a notch below business hotels on the quality level.

There are two other mid-market hotels. One is what is known as an extended stay hotel, which is set up like an apartment or college dorm, with features such as newspaper delivery and kitchenettes in each room. Some extended stay operations serve daily meals, too. Hotels in this sub-category, which include Residence Inn and Homewood Suites, cater to business travelers on long-term assignments, such as architects, engineers, and attorneys.

The third type of mid-market hotel, an all-suite facility, combines elements of several other categories in an effort to reach customers seeking more space for shorter periods of times, from families to business travelers. These hotels, such as Embassy Suites and Clarion Suites, tend to offer a combination of business and mid-market features, including restaurants, cocktail hours, and pools and saunas.

Limited-service hotels: Facilities in this category are limited only in that they tend have few amenities, such as restaurants and large meeting and banquet meeting rooms. However, many of these hotels, which include chains such as Holiday Inn Express, Fairfield Inn, and the Courtyard by Marriott, are located near pockets of restaurants.

The focus of the limited-service hotel segment is to offer clean and comfortable rooms at low rates.

Economy budget hotels: This segment is the flip-side of the luxury segment. These hotels offer little or no features past the actual room, and as such, tend to have the lowest prices. National chains in this segment include Econo Lodge, Super 8, and some Comfort Inns.

One theme throughout these sectors is the presence of chains, which dominate the industry. A REIT, or even an independent hotel operator, can use a chain's features, such as national marketing and advertising; brand reputation; and a centralized reservation system.

Chain standards carry even extra importance for REITs, though, because with few exceptions, REITs are not legally allowed to manage the day-to-day operations of the hotels in their portfolio. If they did, they would be disqualified from being a REIT under the original Real Estate Investment Trust Act of 1960.

Although the REIT Modernization Act of 1999 lightened some restrictions, such as allowing a hotel REIT to form a taxable subsidiary to lease hotels from the REIT, the management company still has to be from an outside company. Using a chain brand, many REIT operators have reasoned, brings some stability into the equation.

Although the name brand of a hotel is a key external factor in the success or failure of hotel REIT, there are several internal management factors that are just as important. First off, a well-capitalized REIT has a considerable advantage over lesser capitalized competitors because the hotel business requires cash infusions to pay for high labor costs and regular renovations.

On a more internal operating basis, a hotel management company has to factor in yield management, a concept similar to what major airlines use in calculating the right combination of price and occupancy levels to reach maximum profits. This concept is how airlines became famous, or in some cases, infamous, for charging dozens of prices for the same flight.

In hotels, the idea is to adjust the price for rooms up and down based on supply-and-demand factors until reaching a predetermined price point. Factors that go into that equation are eliminating vacancies so that no room lies empty. The hotel yield management formula has been aided over the last decade with the proliferation of hotel and travel Web sites that sometimes work out so-called "last minute" deals with hotels.

In total, at the end of 2007, there were ten publicly traded hotel/motel REITs, representing just under 10 percent of all equity REITs. Put together, those 10 REITs held about 15 percent of the entire $200 billion hotel industry. But the choice of brands, management and operation challenges, fluctuating travel demand numbers, and a lack of control over the economy that permeates the entire hotel sector can mean only one thing for hotel REITs and REIT investors: volatility.

Like many other REIT sectors, hotel/motels were on the short end of the volatility charts in 2007, producing a -22.37 percent return for the year, according to the National Association of Real Estate Investment Trusts (NAREIT). A glance at other returns throughout the 2000s further proves the volatility of the sector: In 2003 and 2004, for example, the sector was up 31.7 percent and 32.7 percent, respectively. But in 2001 and 2002 the sector was down 16.3 percent and 1.5 percent, respectively.

Individual Stories

Here is a glimpse inside hotel REITs with four distinct strategies and business models:

COMPANY: ASHFORD HOSPITALITY TRUST

Ticker symbol: AHT; shares are traded on the NYSE

Web site: www.ahtreit.com

Headquarters: Dallas

Founded: 2003

CEO: Montgomery J. Bennett

Revenues: $480.43 million in 2006

Market capitalization: $780.67 million, as of February 23, 2008

Yield: 13.21, as of February 23, 2008

Properties: The company has a stake in more than 120 hotels spread across 30 states, in addition to Canada and the West Indies. Cumulatively, those hotels and motels have more than 15,000 rooms. The company has a variety of brands in its portfolio, too, including Crowne Plaza, DoubleTree, Four Seasons, Hampton Inn, Hilton, Hyatt, JW Marriott, Radisson, Sheraton, and Westin.

Details: Ashford has grown significantly since it initially went public in 2003, when it owned six hotels worth $130 million. Back then, its mission was to invest in distressed hotel properties, starting with four Embassy Suites and a pair of Radissons.

Since then, the company's strategy has evolved to where it now has a position in just about any business cycle that involves the lodging industry. It is one of the largest providers of capital to the hospitality industry, with more than $4 billion in assets.

The strategy starts with owning hotels and motels in multiple markets and of varying quality levels. It continues with providing other companies and hotel operators a variety of investment platforms, including mortgages, mezzanine loans, construction loans, and sale-leaseback transactions. Finally, the company will be part of a deal from either a debt or equity position.

The company says that being both a hotel owner and lender gives it and its executives a broad perspective that is a key factor in any

COMPANY: ASHFORD HOSPITALITY TRUST

deal. Its management team's experience includes being part of selling, financing, operating, and underwriting hotels and motels.

In terms of operating hotels, one of the company's key strategies is to buy hotels in down markets and either continue or undertake a renovation project before the market rebounds. The company says it executed this strategy in California twice in recent years, first with the Hyatt Regency Orange County, which it bought in October 2004 while renovations had already begun.

That hotel, located near Disneyland and the Anaheim Convention Center, had underperformed in its market, the company said. But the hotel has since raised its yield and net operating income levels and increased its year-over-year revenues by 26 percent.

The strategy worked a few hundred miles north of Anaheim, too, with the Pan Pacific Hotel in San Francisco. The company bought that property in 2006 for $95 million and soon after re-branded it a JW Marriott property and spent $10 million on renovations.

The extensive hotel renovations were completed around the same time the San Francisco market, especially in luxury hotels, began to improve. Those factors, in addition to using the Marriott reservation system, have led to that hotel improving its performance, too.

Ashford's top executives, a father-son team, are veterans of the hotel industry. Chairman Archie Bennett Jr. developed his first hotel in Galveston, Texas, in 1968 and since then has been involved in hundreds of hotel projects worth more than $1 billion. Bennett's son, Montgomery Bennett, has also spent his career in the hotel investment industry.

COMPANY: FELCOR LODGING TRUST, INC.

Ticker symbol: FCH; shares are traded on the NYSE

Web site: www.felcor.com

Headquarters: Irving, Texas

Founded: 1991; company went public in 1994.

CEO: Rick Smith

Revenues: $991.04 million in 2006

Market capitalization: $761.77 million, as of February 23, 2008

Yield: 11.48, as of February 23, 2008

Properties: The company's 85-hotel portfolio is spread across 23 states and Canada and is made up mostly of high-end brands, such as Embassy Suites, Hilton, and Westin. The company's location strategy is to have hotels near the downtown or airports of major markets, including Atlanta, Dallas, Los Angeles, Orlando, Phoenix, San Diego, San Francisco, and Washington, D.C.

Details: FelCor, with a $2.9 billion hotel portfolio, is one of the largest hotel REITs in the country.

The company has grown significantly since its 1994 public offering, when it had six hotels in its portfolio and a market capitalization of about $120 million. The 2008 version of the company is a showcase in how important it is for hotel REITs to be well capitalized.

For example, the company recently began renovating each of its core hotel properties, a project it says will cost more than $430 million, or about $20,000 per room. The renovation projects are comprehensive in scale, with plans to hit on all of a property's guest rooms, guest bathrooms, public areas, meeting spaces and conference rooms, roofing, and other exterior areas. The project is expected to be completed by the middle of 2008, the company reported on its Web site early that year.

The company has also been working on a redevelopment program to add components such as extra meeting space, guest rooms, and spas to a select group of properties. In total, FelCor identified 14

COMPANY: FELCOR LODGING TRUST, INC.

hotels in its portfolio for this program, which is expected to cost about $150 million. Projects underway as of 2007 include adding meeting space to a hotel in Dana Point, California, and building a new convention center in Myrtle Beach, next to a Hilton hotel the company owns. The redevelopment program also includes an effort to develop condos on excess land the company controls near some of its beachfront properties.

The renovation and redevelopment programs follow another company-wide effort designed to reposition the company, only this one was designed to bring in money, not spend it. That is, beginning in 2006, FelCor worked out a deal with one if its partners in the hotel business, InterContinental, to sell all of its Holiday Inn properties in secondary locations it no longer wanted to be in. The company identified 45 hotels as non-strategic, a portfolio worth $715 million.

The company planned to use some of the proceeds from those sales to fund the renovation and redevelopment project, in addition to paying off debt incurred from some other projects.

COMPANY: SUPERTEL

Ticker symbol: SPPR; shares are traded on the NASDAQ

Web site: www.supertelinc.com

Headquarters: Norfolk, Nebraska

Founded: 1994; changed name from Humphrey Hospitality Trust, Inc. to Supertel Hospitality, Inc. in 2005.

CEO: Paul J. Schulte

Revenues: $77.32 million in 2006

Market capitalization: $120.5 million, as of February 23, 2008

Yield: 8.70, as of February 23, 2008

Properties: The company controls a portfolio of 125 properties spread across 24 states in the limited service and economy subsectors of the hotel market. Brand names in the portfolio include Comfort Inn/Comfort Suites, Days Inn, Hampton Inn, Holiday Inn Express,

COMPANY: SUPERTEL

Ramada, and Super 8. Most of the company's hotels, which total about 11,000 rooms, are in the Midwest and Southeast United States, with a few properties in the Pacific Northwest and New England.

Supertel's portfolio has grown significantly in the past few years. In 2007, it bought 27 properties, and in just the first month of 2008 it bought 10 more properties, including 7 in Kentucky.

Details: The company's growth strategy for its portfolio revolves around finding locations near industrial business sectors, government and military bases, and some colleges and universities, where demand for lower-priced hotel rooms is higher than it is in downtowns or outside high-traffic airports.

The company also seeks some resort locations to develop or buy properties, as a way to provide a lower-cost alternative to some of the high-end properties there. Another niche the company has found is in buying properties in markets with an aging hotel sector.

From a financing perspective, the company strives to maintain a low leverage of long-term debt to investments, something in the 40-55 percent range. It then seeks 60-70 percent leverage on acquisitions, through both current and new credit lines.

Supertel has found that operating in the economy and limited-service sector of the hotel industry has some advantages, even though the price points do not compare to luxury or even business hotels. For instance, the 2007 credit markets debacle could result in people seeking lower-priced hotels for business and leisure trips.

Also, Supertel's chairman, president, and chief executive officer, Paul J. Schulte, said the nationwide economic and credit market problems could ultimately turn into an opportunity for the company. "We do not expect the recent difficulties experienced in the credit market to have a significant impact on Supertel," Schulte said in the company's 2007 third-quarter earning statement, issued November

COMPANY: SUPERTEL

8, 2007. "In fact, it may increase the pool of properties available for acquisitions as some owners who will need to refinance may not be able to obtain debt at the same attractive interest rates as that of the past few years."

COMPANY: LASALLE HOTEL PROPERTIES

Ticker symbol: LHO; shares are traded on the NYSE

Web site: www.lasallehotels.com

Headquarters: Bethesda, Maryland

Founded: 1998

CEO: Jon E. Bortz

Revenues: $626.85 million in 2006

Market capitalization: $1.16 billion, as of February 23, 2008

Yield: 7.03, as of February 23, 2008

Properties: The company owns 31 upscale luxury hotels and resorts in 14 markets spread across 11 states and Washington, D.C. The portfolio, which consists of about 8,500 rooms, is broken down into 20 urban properties, six resorts, and five convention hotels.

Its urban hotels include the Hotel Deca in Seattle's University District, the Hotel Helix in downtown Washington, D.C., and the Onyx Hotel in downtown Boston. Resorts include the San Diego Paradise Point Resort & Spa, and convention properties include the Westin Michigan Avenue in Chicago and the Indianapolis Marriott Downtown.

Details: Jon Bortz, the original president and chief executive officer of LaSalle Hotel Properties, brought some top-notch experience to the company when he joined it in 1998: he previously founded and oversaw the hotel group of Jones Lang LaSalle, Inc. a Chicago-based real estate conglomerate. In that role, Bortz ran all of the company's hotel investment and development activities.

One major component to LaSalle Hotel Properties' strategy is that the company buys and invests in only high-end luxury

COMPANY: LASALLE HOTEL PROPERTIES

properties where it can provide guests with more than just a bed and a shower. Many of its hotel rooms and lobbies are uniquely designed to fit the culture and life style of that particular city.

Another integral component to LaSalle Hotel Properties' strategy is that the company, according to its Web site, strives to be made up of professional hotel investors, asset managers, and financial experts, not merely hotel operators.

As far as its actual hotel investments, the company says it seeks hotels and resorts in markets where the barriers to new supply are high and luxury room demand is both strong and predictable. It also will undertake renovation and upgrade programs for certain hotels and properties in high-demand markets.

The company has steadily grown its hotel portfolio over the last decade, beginning with 10 properties in 1998. Since then, the company has participated in several multimillion-dollar deals, either to buy, sell, or partner with another entity on a hotel project. One of the more recent examples of a LaSalle Hotel Properties transaction was in 2007, when the company sold the LaGuardia Marriott, a deal that brought in a $30.4 million net gain.

The company also has set up a tiered strategy to lower risk and maintains a solid balance sheet. From a risk perspective, the company's initiatives include geographic diversification, as its markets include Boston, San Diego, and Seattle; property type diversification; using multiple hotel operators; and partnering with independent hotel owners and nationally known brands such as Hyatt, Sheraton, and Westin.

Meanwhile, its balance sheet strategy includes focusing on maintaining low leverage, using variable and fixed-rate debt to hedge the economic cycle, using unsecured debt to add flexibility, and staggering debt maturities.

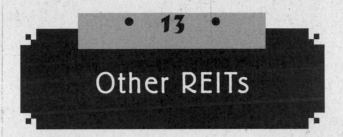

Other REITs

When it comes to REITs, the word "other" can be broad. But the big players in this category can be broken down into three sections: specialty REITs, diversified REITs, and mortgage REITs.

A fourth category is what is known as hybrid REITs, which combines a mortgage REIT operation with an equity REIT operation. These structures have become less popular over the years, to the point where only a few healthcare REITs are still considered hybrids.

But the first two categories, specialty and diversified, are still pure equity REITs, which means the companies own and operate real estate properties. The revenues, and it follows, the dividend paid out to shareholders, come primarily from rents and fees earned from renting out property, from a hotel room to a warehouse to a doctor's office.

Mortgage REITs, on the other hand, loan money to other real estate companies or outright purchase existing mortgages and mortgage-backed securities. A mortgage REIT's revenues stem primarily from interest earned on the mortgage loans.

Specialty REITs

Specialty REITs have an everything-left-over feel. But that does not necessarily mean the occupants of this sector are trash. Instead, the six publicly traded specialty REITs are well, special. The list of specialty REITs at one time or another has included companies owning and operating automobile dealerships, gas stations, golf courses, movie theaters, prisons, timber companies, and even a business that rents rooftops for wireless communications companies.

Nonetheless, although the list is indeed special, the sector has mostly been treated as an afterthought in the REIT world. Essentially, because the businesses overseen by specialty REITs do not normally fit squarely into the mainstream, there is a lack of understanding, which sometimes translates to lack of interest.

From a performance standpoint, specialty REITs have had a solid return rate in the past decade, including a 38.6 percent return in 2003 and a 26.9 percent return in 2004. Even in 2007, while many other REITs were struggling, the specialty REIT sector produced a 14.56 percent return, according to the National Association of Real Estate Investment Trusts (NAREIT).

As of the beginning of 2008, two specialty REITs were so special, that there was no other REIT like them in the marketplace. One, San Rafael, California-based Vintage Wine Trust, invests in vineyards and other wine industry assets, such as crushing, processing, and storage facilities. The winery-based REIT also has a segment devoted to financing arrangements with branded wineries, bulk wine producers, and independent grape growers in the United States and Canada.

Another ultra-special REIT operating in 2008, Kansas City-based Entertainment Properties Trust, invested in $2 billion-plus worth of high-end entertainment properties, including movie megaplexes, ski resorts, and water parks.

Historically though, specialty REITs have followed business trends. This was especially evident in the early 1990s, when golf course REITs began generating high expectations. And for good reason: the golf course industry was saddled with several operating characteristics that REIT operators and investors tend to find attractive.

For example, its positive demographic and growth lines and its primary end user came to the market with deep pockets. The number of golfers nationwide doubled from the early 1980s through 1995, from 16 million to 32 million. During the same time, however, golf courses were growing only at a 10 percent rate.

In the supply-and-demand world of REITs, that could only mean one thing: opportunity.

Another specialty REIT that has historically followed the business trends is that of prisons and jails. This trend developed in the 1990s, as state and local governments began getting out of the prison and jail business and bringing in private companies to do the work.

Companies such as Correctional Properties Trust, Prison Realty Trust, Correctional Properties, and Prison Realty were a good fit for these government entities. The companies provided staff, from wardens to line correction officers, and saved the government money while capitalizing on the trend to privatize tasks normally associated with the government.

Meanwhile, on the REIT side of things, prison REITs, for a time early this decade, attracted a small cult-like following in the REIT community, as the companies delivered a modest, bond-type yield with little risk.

The golf course and prison REIT trend was short-lived: as of 2007, there was no longer any publicly traded equity REITs in either category, according to NAREIT. Of course, market conditions could change in the future, and golf course and prison REITs could return.

More REITs

Mortgage REITs have also lost some of their luster over the years, although the category has not completely dried out. Indeed, as of 2008, there were 25 companies tracked by NAREIT's Mortgage REIT index.

Still, that is a long way from the late 1960s and the early 1970s, when mortgage REITs dominated the entire industry. More than 60 mortgage REITs were formed back then, as bankers and mortgage brokers sought ways to capitalize on high-interest-rate loans to contractors and developers.

But by 1973, when the construction industry began entering an overbuilding phase and interest rates were getting too high for most companies, the mortgage REIT industry began to slide. Many of those early mortgage REITs simply went out of business, while others switched focus.

The mortgage REIT sector returned to a more prominent position in the 1990s, to capitalize on a yet another real estate and building boom. Over the last decade or so, mortgage REITs have found a new niche: nonconforming loans.

These nonconforming loans, either commercial or residential, are too complicated, or sometimes, too troubled, to be part of a pool of mortgage-backed securities that are flipped and sold on the mortgage-backed securities market. Most banks and standard lenders will not partake in the nonconforming loan market, due to the high risk.

Mortgage REITs, just like equity REITs, have subsectors. As of 2008, for instance, there were 10 home-financing REITs and 15 commercial-financing REITs, according to NAREIT. Although today's mortgage REITs aim to have more stability and staying power, from an investment standpoint, mortgage REITs are considerably more risky than equity REITs.

First, mortgage REITs, by nature are heavily dependent on interest rates and as such are even more connected to economic cycles than most equity REITs. The late-2007 and early 2008 interest rate cuts, for example, put a strain on mortgage REITs. To wit: the sector produced a -42.35 percent return in 2007, according to NAREIT.

Mortgage REITs are also, by nature, connected to debt-laden deals. That increases the leverage, which in turn adds a high volatility component to a REIT's earnings and dividends. Moreover, since mortgage REITs do not own or control property, judging its financial prospects is more of a guessing game.

Although specialty and mortgage REITs are aptly named, diversified REITs are a misnomer in one way: these REITs might have a diverse portfolio, but from a geography perspective, they tend to stick to one location of the country, such as the Southeast or New England.

By sticking to one geographic market of a region, even a large one, the goal of these types of REITs is to become proficient in the area's entire real estate market, not just office or housing or hotels. The REIT operators can then leverage that knowledge into acquisitions, deals, and other opportunities.

As of 2008, there were eight publicly traded diversified REITs. Not unlike other REIT sectors, the diversified sector struggled in 2007, producing a -22.29 percent return, according to NAREIT. For prior years of the past decade, the diversified sector was significantly volatile: it was up a meager 1.5 percent in 2002, followed by a resounding 40.3 percent return in 2003 and a still robust 32.4 percent return in 2004.

Diversified REITs though, as a sector, had some trouble in past years. In the 1970s and 1980s, diversified REITs had a scattered focus both in geography and product type; a few were hybrid REITs, owning property and mortgages at the same time. That lack of focus proved to be dangerous when the construction industry suffered through an overbuilding period in the late 1980s and early 1990s, as many of those original diversified REITs struggled.

Some of those troubled REITs were in such bad shape that the operators were not able to pay a dividend, forcing them to give up their REIT status. Great Neck, New York-based BRT Realty, for example, which started out as a mortgage REIT in the 1970s before becoming a diversified REIT, was forced to drop its REIT status from 1990 through 1996. The company has since regained REIT status and now operates as a mortgage REIT.

Individual Stories

Here is a glimpse inside four non-mainstream equity REITs with distinct strategies and business models:

COMPANY: COLONIAL PROPERTIES TRUST (DIVERSIFIED)

Ticker symbol: CLP; shares are traded on the NYSE

Web site: www.colonialprop.com

Headquarters: Birmingham, Alabama

Founded: 1970; company went public in 1993

CEO: C. Reynolds Thompson, III

Revenues: $445.38 million in 2006

Market capitalization: $1.19 billion, as of February 23, 2008

Yield: 7.97, as of February 23, 2008

Properties: The company's diversified portfolio has a far reach, with three sectors taking up a lot space: multifamily housing, office, and retail properties. The company operates mostly in Sunbelt states, such as Florida and Georgia, but it also has properties in states as far north as Maryland and as far west as California and Arizona.

In the multifamily sector, the company owns more than 140 apartment communities, which total more than 39,000 apartments. In the office market, the company has a controlling stake in 53 properties that are composed of nearly 17 million square feet of office space. As of 2007, the company's multifamily, office, and retail properties had occupancy levels of 95.5 percent, 93.5 percent, and 93.1 percent, respectively.

Details: With such a diverse business model, Colonial Properties needs to have several different programs and deals working at once to succeed. One of the company's ongoing goals, therefore, is that on a quarterly and annual basis, these programs lead to improved short-term and long-term financial results.

For example, according to the Colonial's 2007 fourth quarter and year-end earnings release, the company achieved the following benchmarks in 2007:

COMPANY: COLONIAL PROPERTIES TRUST (DIVERSIFIED)

- Achieved multifamily same-property net operating income growth of 5.2 percent.

- Ended the year with same-property physical occupancy of 96.1 percent.

- Improved the quality of its multifamily portfolio through the sale of 3,489 wholly owned apartment homes with an average of 20 years.

- Completed a strategic plan to focus core operations on multifamily business.

- Contributed 24 office and 2 retail properties into a joint venture with a total transaction value of $1.13 billion.

- Contributed 11 retail properties into joint venture with a total transaction value of $360 million.

- Sold 16 non-core retail assets outright for $265.8 million.

- Recognized $17 million or $0.30 per diluted share in net income and funds from operations (FFO) gains from commercial development and for-sale residential activities.

- Recognized $3.3 million, or $0.06 per diluted share in net income and FFO gains from sales of land and out-parcels.

- Completed development and announced full leasing of Colonial Center Brookwood, a 160,000-square-foot Class A office complex in Colonial Brookwood Village in Birmingham, Alabama.

- Reduced leverage (debt plus preferred stock as a percentage of underappreciated book value) by 310 basis points from December 31, 2006, to 57.7 percent at February 23, 2008.

The company is planning to grow some of its divisions, too, on an individual basis. For example, the company's office space division,

COMPANY: COLONIAL PROPERTIES TRUST (DIVERSIFIED)

based out of suburban Atlanta, seeks joint venture projects in high-job growth Sunbelt cities, such as Nashville and Raleigh, North Carolina.

The company is looking for deals involving multi-tenant office buildings built between 1985 and 2006 that are either Class A or Class B and 100,000 square feet or larger. The company says it will consider deals worth $15 million to $300 million and one distinct advantage it has over competitors is that it buys its properties using cash to avoid financing issues, thus ensuring a quick closing.

COMPANY: CAPITAL TRUST, INC. (MORTGAGE)

Ticker symbol: CT; shares are traded on the NYSE

Web site: www.capitaltrust.com

Headquarters: New York City

Founded: 1997; company took on REIT status in 2003

CEO: John R. Klopp

Revenues: $77.46 million in 2006

Market capitalization: $496.01 million, as of February 23, 2008

Yield: 11.57, as of February 23, 2008

Properties: As a mortgage REIT, the company does not outright own or operate any real estate holdings. In terms of loans, however, the company has closed on more than $10 billion worth of mezzanine loans and other investments in more than 500 separate transactions.

Details: Capital Trust focuses on investments in the commercial real estate industry, where its executives and board of directors are considered to be some of the best in the industry.

The list includes company cofounder and chairman Sam Zell, who runs a separate well-known Chicago-based real estate company in addition to his work at Capital Trust. Zell is also well known for

COMPANY: CAPITAL TRUST, INC. (MORTGAGE)

buying the Tribune Media Co. in 2007; the company owns several national newspapers, such as the *Chicago Tribune* and the *Los Angels Times*, as well as the Chicago Cubs baseball team.

Capital Trust's chief executive officer, John Klopp, who co-founded the firm with Zell, previously worked in executive positions with Chemical Banking and Chemical Realty Corp.

The company, in addition to having a star-studded list of executives and board members, focuses on five loan and investment areas, including:

- **Property mezzanine investments:** These are high-yielding loans and other investments that are loans, such as second mortgages, on commercial real estate properties. The loans, the company says, represent a subordinate interest in a first mortgage, a second mortgage, a pledge of ownership interest in the borrowing property owner, or a preferred equity interest in the property owner.

The company's property mezzanine investments range in value from $10 million to $100 million and last about 3 to 5 years. The company says it will consider property mezzanine investments for any property type and in any geographic market.

Finally, at times, the company originates and closes whole loans in which it intends to sell a senior debt portion and keep the junior debt portion, thereby creating a property mezzanine investment.

- **Transitional mortgage loans:** These are senior and junior mortgage loans that are secured by properties requiring interim financing until a sale or permanent financing is worked out. The company's minimum for this type of loan is $25 million, and the loans are short-term, lasting about one to three years. Like the company's property mezzanine investments, these loans are open to all property types and geographic markets.

COMPANY: CAPITAL TRUST, INC. (MORTGAGE)

- **Corporate mezzanine investments:** These investments are loans to real estate operating companies, including REITs. In addition to a loan, the company says these investments could take the form of secured or unsecured debt, preferred stock, and other hybrid instruments such as convertible debt, which are bonds in a company that can later be converted to shares. In turn, the company's corporate mezzanine investments can perform a number of features for the company borrowing the money, including finance mergers and acquisitions, management buy-outs, and startups.

The company provides corporate mezzanine investments only when it is for real estate or a real estate-related entity.

Capital Trust's two other loan and investment areas are determined on a case-by-case basis, depending on the location, size, and several internal and external economic factors.

COMPANY: ONE LIBERTY PROPERTIES, INC. (DIVERSIFIED)

Ticker symbol: OLP; shares are traded on the NYSE

Web site: www.1liberty.com

Headquarters: Great Neck, New York

Founded: 1982

CEO: Patrick J. Callan Jr.

Revenues: $33.37 million in 2006

Market capitalization: $175.34 million, as of February 23, 2008

Yield: 8.34, as of February 23, 2008

Properties: The company owns close to 70 properties spread across 28 states, totaling more than 5.9 million square feet. Its holdings at one time included retail, residential, industrial, office, movie theater, and health and fitness facilities. The company also has ownership stakes in properties held through joint ventures and tenant in common partnerships, which a form of joint ownership of commercial real estate properties.

COMPANY: ONE LIBERTY PROPERTIES, INC. (DIVERSIFIED)

Details: Although One Liberty Properties has one of the most diverse portfolios of any REIT on the market in terms of property type, its business focus is singular: signing tenants to net leases where the tenant is responsible to pay a bulk of the costs necessary to keep a property operating at full capacity.

These costs include real estate taxes, maintenance, insurance, and utilities. The benefit of this type of lease structure is that it facilitates long-term cash flow stability because the tenant pays the spikes in certain costs, such as property taxes.

Plus, the company's leases tend to have two other features. One is that the leases are written on a long-term basis, to ensure stability through short-term economic downturns. For instance, excluding leases connected to properties the company holds in joint ventures, more than 80 percent of its leases expire after 2012, and another 55 percent expire after 2016.

The second feature of most of the company's leases is scheduled rate increase clauses. More than 90 percent of the company's entire lease portfolio in 2007 had either scheduled rent increases or consumer price index-based rate hikes written into the contracts, according to a 2007 filing with the Securities and Exchange Commission. Much like long-term leases, these clauses give the company a cushion if certain parts of the economy or its markets begin faltering.

The company has spread this lease strategy among all of its clients. On a national retail basis, that includes Barnes & Noble, Walgreens, The Sports Authority, Best Buy, Circuit City, Petco, and TGI Friday's.

Like most of the other REITs that undertake a net lease philosophy, One Liberty is completely behind the strategy. On the company's Web site, it states that its "emphasis on property value enables us to achieve better returns on our acquired properties and also enhances our ability to re-rent or dispose of a property on

COMPANY: ONE LIBERTY PROPERTIES, INC. (DIVERSIFIED)

favorable terms on the expiration or early termination of a lease."

The company regularly seeks new tenants and acquisitions where it can use its lease strategy. It looks for properties with a base value of at least $5 million and is open to just about any property type, including office, warehouse, manufacturing, retail, stadium-style movie theaters, and fast-food restaurants. From a geographic perspective, the company will consider any part of the United States, as long as a property is in a high-traffic area with easy access to major highways.

COMPANY: RAYONIER (SPECIALTY)

Ticker symbol: RYN; shares are traded on the NYSE

Web site: www.rayonier.com

Headquarters: Jacksonville, Florida

Founded: 1926; company went public in 1994 and reorganized as an equity REIT in 2004

CEO: Lee M. Thomas

Revenues: $1.229 billion in 2006

Market capitalization: $3.30 billion, as of February 23, 2008

Yield: 4.74, as of February 23, 2008

Properties: The company owns, leases, or manages about 2.6 million acres of timber and land in the United States and New Zealand.

In addition, through TerraPointe LLC, its development subsidiary, the company owns 200,000 acres of property that could be put together for a variety of uses, including commercial and residential development, conservation, or public infrastructure. Most of that land is located in a 200-mile radius of the company's North Florida headquarters, in coastal towns and counties from Savannah, Georgia south to Daytona Beach, Florida.

Details: Rayonier has three distinct business divisions: Timber, estate, and performance fibers.

COMPANY: RAYONIER (SPECIALTY)

Outside the REIT investing world, the company is known for its timber business, which stretches nine states in the United States in addition to New Zealand. The timber is ultimately grown and sold for use by paper, pulp, and lumber manufacturers in the United States and the Asian Pacific region.

The company's timber strategy follows a REIT strategy of diversification. That is, the company seeks out forests and timber properties that have varied economic cycles so as to not rely on the ups and downs of one market.

Hence, the company owns and operates forests and other related properties as far away from Florida as Auckland, New Zealand. That is the headquarters for the company's Pacific Forest Resources unit, which, in a joint venture with a New Zealand plantation company, manages 350,000-plus acres of timberland. About 70 percent of the forest's harvest is sold to New Zealand mills for lumber processing, with the other 30 percent going to other East Asian markets.

Considerably closer to the United States is Rayonier's Eastern Forest Resources and Western Forest Resources divisions. The Eastern Forest unit is based in Fernandina Beach, Florida, near the company's corporate office, and it manages about 1.8 million acres of timberland spread across eight states, from New York to Texas. The timber products include hardwoods, sugar maple, black cherry, and red spruce.

The Western Forest unit, meanwhile, manages about 370,000 acres of timberland and is based out of Hoquiam, Washington, on the Pacific Coast. Those lands produce a mixed species of conifers, Douglas fir, and western red cedar.

Rayonier's real estate arm, TerraPointe LLC, was formed in 2005 as a way to capitalize on growing population trends in the Southeast United States, where the company operates a bulk of its Eastern forest properties. The thinking was that it could turn a larger

COMPANY: RAYONIER (SPECIALTY)

profit on selling some of that land for development, recreation, or conservation purposes, as opposed to using it only for forestry.

The company's third major business division, performance fibers, is considered one of the leading producers of specialty cellulose fibers in the world. Companies use the fibers to manufacture a variety of products, including LCD screens for TVs and computers, paints, cosmetics, textile, and impact-resistant plastics.

Finally, separate from its business units, Rayonier has some political star power at the top executive level: Lee Thomas, who was named president and chief executive officer of Rayonier in 2007, served as administrator of the U.S. Environmental Protection Agency from 1985-1989. President Ronald Reagan appointed Thomas the position.

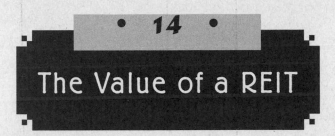

14

The Value of a REIT

The residential real estate market collapse of 2007, a situation that began threatening the value of many commercial properties early in 2008, proves that gauging the true value of a piece of property is a difficult game. There are many opinions on the right way to do it but little consensus among the so-called experts.

It holds then, that judging the valuation of REITs would be a complicated process, too. Although that may be so, there are still a few established ways of looking at the inner workings of a REIT's financials to get to the most important part from an investor's standpoint: will this REIT outperform the other stocks in the portfolio, and will it outperform the stock market?

Before taking a look at the unique aspects of the metrics and measurements of a REIT, it makes sense to look at a few ways of measuring the value of real estate. The three most established methods of judging the value of a piece of real estate are the replacement cost method, the market comparable approach, and a capitalization rate valuation.

The replacement cost method does just that: it figures out, or at least attempts to figure out, what it would cost in the current market to replace or replicate a building of a similar size and rating quality in a similar location.

A replacement cost study can be, and should be, a detailed analysis. It includes the value of the land the building occupies, site improvements, and a understanding of the neighborhood that surrounds the property.

The details though, can go only so far. Because every commercial building is unique and has positive, or sometimes negative, features, it is difficult for a replacement cost study to be anything more than a rough generalization.

Sill, the replacement cost method fits snugly with a second valuation methodology, the market comparable approach. This is a study of sales of similar buildings in the general location of the given property.

Just like the replacement cost method, this concept, when working independently, tends to provide only generalities. For example, the data is based on recent historic sales reports, but it could miss some new changes to the marketplace. Also, even more important, the price of a building sale used in a historical analysis could be skewed by the needs of the individual buyer and seller: maybe the seller has some pressing need to sell the property due to personal or business circumstances and will accept and offer lower than the market rate. Or maybe the buyer is willing to pay a premium for the property because the building has one or more features uniquely suited to his or her business.

Because those elements complicate the market comparison study, it makes sense to study a wider range of building and property values, to come up with an average price. Of course, straying too far outside a commercial real estate market could lead to another skewing of the data by bringing too many variables into the equation.

From an individual investor's standpoint, there is one constant positive element to either a replacement cost method or the market comparable approach: access. Most towns, counties, and cities have used the Internet to create databases of property sales and other information that are easy to navigate.

A third established method for judging the value of a given piece of real estate is the capitalization of net income, or, simply, the cap rate. As explained in Chapter 3, a cap rate is a method of determining a commercial real estate property's risk level. It is determined by dividing a property's post-expenses net operating income by its purchase price.

The higher the cap rate, the higher the return potential as well as the risk. The lower the cap rate, the lower the perceived risk. Therefore, a property with an annual net operating income of $100,000 and an asking price of $1 million would have a 10 percent cap rate.

The cap rate of a commercial property can be a base point for judging the value of other buildings in a given market. The larger the market, the more relevant the cap rate becomes in studying building valuations, because it allows for a broader analysis.

Because all three valuations have positive and negative features, it makes sense to use all three when studying a building. But even when using all three methodologies, many building and property appraisers will say the work is just as much an art as it is a science.

Operational Funds

There are even more methodologies for gauging the value of a company or a company's stock. Unlike the measurements used for gauging real estate property, there is one method that, for general purposes, is universally accepted as the best way of measuring a stock's value.

That measurement is a company's income and/or its cash flow. This is because, simply, a company with a rising income and cash flow has more opportunities to grow in other areas, from research and development to purchasing, and that growth could lead to a higher stock price.

This formula, time-tested in the stock market for decades, has some twists when it is introduced to REITs. This is because a REIT's sole product— real estate —has a singularly unique valuation method, as noted in the preceding part of this chapter.

Therefore, the valuation of a REIT stock begins with examining the company's funds from operations (FFO). Essentially, a REIT's FFO is the net income a REIT generates, excluding gains or losses from sales of property and adding back real estate depreciation. When compared to normal corporate accounting, it is a good approximation of cash flow and considered to be an even better judge of operations than the standard for U.S. public companies: generally accepted accounting principles (GAAP).

The FFO accounting method was created during the REIT boom of the early 1990s, as investors and REIT operators saw the need to have a standardized system that looked at appreciation properly. A few years later, the term adjusted funds from operations was created, which is essentially a REIT's FFO adjusted for the expenditures that do little to enhance the value of a property and is adjusted further by eliminating the cost of straight-lining rents; the Newport Beach, California-based REIT research firm Green Street Advisors, is widely credited with creating the AFFO measurement tool.

The nature of a company's cash flow — its revenues minus its costs — is the most important part of the equation, whether looking at FFO, AFFO, or both. For a REIT, costs can be operating expenses, administrative costs, financial costs, and capital expenses. Specifically, those costs could be anything from leases to new drapes in an apartment or from new carpets for an office to debt payments.

For an investor's purposes, a REIT's FFO is significantly more meaningful than a company's net income or cash flow. This is because real estate depreciation is treated as an expense under GAAP rules, and it shows up that way on a company's balance sheet that way under cash flow.

But in reality, most real estate property appreciates over time, not depreciates. This is because a well-maintained property with other quality feature and amenities can go up in value over the years; at least an investor hopes it does, otherwise there would be no reason to invest in it. Other factors that can lead to appreciation, not depreciation, include increasing land values on and near where the building is built, rising rents, and higher costs for competing properties.

It is for this reason that analysts, investors, and REIT operators and executives agree: a REIT's FFO is a more meaningful than its income or cash flow.

Although that might sound simple, and for the most part, it is, there are some complications. For example, the formula and definition of what comprises a REIT's FFO is not a settled science.

The confusion around calculating a REIT's FFO stems from the lack of a consistency in reporting standards. The REIT industry's largest trade organization and lobbying group, the National Association of Real Estate Investment Trusts (NAREIT), has spent the past decade tinkering with the system to create a more standard method. Indeed, in 1995 and then again in 1999, NAREIT published a pair of white papers calling for a few changes to the FFO accounting methodology.

One big area that has led to confusion in calculating FFO is in the accounting of nonrecurring items. This is because a REIT is allowed to add back any items its executive and accountants consider to be nonrecurring, which would not be allowed under GAAP.

The result is that some REITs take advantage of this rule by aggressively searching for items that can be considered nonrecurring. Those items include employee severance packages, public relations and advertising costs, failed acquisitions, and losses on interest rate hedging deals.

Meanwhile, other REITs consider those costs ongoing business expenses, which not only leads to confusion but difficulty in comparing REIT balance sheets.

Another area of FFO accounting that has caused confusion for

REIT investors is in gains and losses from deals such as debt restructuring and property sales. This is because some REITs are more ambitious in seeking to count the gains from the transactions on its FFO, thereby potentially fostering a skewed reading of the FFO.

The FFO accounting method used by all REITs has a few other flaws, too. For instance, a commercial property, by nature, depreciates over years of wear and tear. A property might also require certain repairs, such as new roof or other structural improvements. Therefore, adding back deprecation to net income, which is routinely done under FFO, might paint an overly optimistic picture of a REIT's cash flow and balance sheet.

Just like figuring out makes up a nonrecurring item, other problems with FFO accounting revolve around what constitutes depreciation. For instance, some REITs count short-term fixes to properties, say window treatments on an apartment building, as a capital improvement that would qualify as deprecation on a balance sheet. Other REITs might not account for depreciation in the same way, again bringing inconsistency into the picture.

Growth Methods

Despite the accounting imperfections inherent in an FFO, it remains the best way an investor can judge a REIT's profitability. But to judge a long-term value of a REIT, not just how profitable it was for a given quarter, it is essential to monitor how a REIT grows its FFO.

If a REIT is not growing its FFO, it becomes the equivalent of a yield-producing bond. Not that there is anything wrong with a bond, per se, but investors pay a premium for a REIT stock and as such expect a high return in addition high yields and consistent dividends.

On paper, a REIT's FFO growth equation is simple: add internal growth with external growth, and the result is FFO growth. In that way, it is similar to other publicly traded companies seeking growth through a combination of internal operations and outside acquisitions.

In theory though, a REIT's FFO growth process is more complicated. External growth, which can come from areas such as new building purchases, new markets, and new developments, is somewhat out of a REIT operator's control. This is because of the ever-changing capital markets and the high cost of capital that sometimes makes deals an inefficient use of capital.

Meanwhile, internal growth, also refereed to as organic growth, is something a REIT executive has more control over but is also hard to obtain on a consistent basis. This is because internal growth relies not only on a sound strategy but execution of that strategy, which takes talented people working in the right positions.

A REIT seeks internal growth by using the concept known in retail as same-store sales. That is a measurement that monitors the sales from stores open at least one year, excluding stores that are new, as those tend to have higher sales from having just opened.

For REIT investors, and not just those looking into retail REITs, the same-store sales concept is important because it provides a clear picture of how the REIT is doing with its portfolio as compared to both its own history and other REITs. In REITs, the concept is easily translated to same-store rental revenues, which can include office, residential, and warehouse space, among other property types.

Some REITs are more aggressive than others in seeking same-store rental revenue growth, and those REITs tend to have faster internal growth rates. But there are factors in the internal growth equation, too, beyond simply wanting it real bad. Location and quality of the properties counts for a lot, as does the market conditions surrounding the property.

Internal growth strategies include:

Rental Revenue Increases

The ability to raise rents is the best and the most obvious way to facilitate internal growth. But reaching a point where raising rents is feasible on a regular basis can be difficult, as many other factors are involved. Those include vacancies in the market; the market economy; supply-and-demand forces, including overbuilding; and the changing needs of the tenant, such as downsizing.

Each REIT sector has its own rent-raising formulas, but self-storage facilities and retail REITs have had the easiest time raising rents between 2003 and 2008. This is primarily because the supply level, especially in self-storage, has not outstripped the demand. Some experts predict that the apartment market might be the next place to see an increase in rents, the result of the housing slowdown forcing millions of people out of homes and into apartments.

Expense Sharing

This concept, also known as cost recovery, is when a landlord, or in this case a REIT operator, gets the tenants in any given property to share expenses that at one time were covered by the landlord. This can take the form of having office and retail tenants pay for maintenance of common areas, or in apartments, it could be adding separate water and heating meters to each apartment so that the tenant controls and pays for his or her own utilities.

The rub, of course, in expense sharing, is in the leverage of convincing tenants to pay for something they previously weren't paying for. Some of the biggest REITs use their size in getting tenants to agree to cost sharing, while others use old-fashioned relationship-based sales techniques.

Rent Bumps

These are primarily used by REITs in sectors that require long-term leases, such as office, industrial, and healthcare REITs. The bump is a clause built into the original lease contract that calls for periodic increases in the rent. The increases can be based on a number of factors, such as inflation increases.

Retail REITs also sometimes write in rate bumps to leases to match the rates with the expected increase in a store's revenues.

Percentage Rent

Used primarily within the retail REIT sector and also known as a breakpoint, this concept allows the landlord, or, in this case, the REIT operator, to receive a prenegotiated amount of cash from the retailer if that retailer reaches a certain point in sales. The landlord agrees to do things — at his own cost — to drum up business for the retailer, such as putting up signs, advertising, and promotional events. In turn, the retailer agrees to kick back a percentage of the sales.

Property Improvements

This concept, while simple in theory, is costly and time consuming in practice. That sometimes puts it at the bottom of the list of potential ways to improve the internal growth aspects of a REIT's FFO. But a successful improvement or renovation project of a property, from an office building to a shopping mall to an apartment complex, could lead to a rebirth in the property and, it follows, higher rents.

Tenant Upgrades

Just like percentage rents, this concept is used mostly in retail REITs. Within malls and shopping centers, it involves a game of figuring out what store will do better in a certain location. Then it takes recruiting that store, if it is not currently in the market, to come to that specific shopping mall and sometimes even phasing current stores out of the mall.

This concept is especially important in tough economic times, where more stores are on the verge of failing. During times like that, it is crucial to have the right mix of stores.

Reinvestment

Also refereed to as capital recycling, this concept follows the strategy of selling underperforming properties to use proceeds from those sales to invest in other, higher-margin buildings. In REIT accounting, this concept is still considered internal growth because the new projects are funded by the sale of properties already in the REIT's portfolio and do not require new loans or other sources of financing.

Although the internal growth aspects of a REIT's FFO are essential, the external growth components of a REIT's FFO can not be ignored. This is because no matter how strong a REIT's internal growth mechanisms are, achieving top-tier FFO growth requires some external growth, too. The main methods of external growth are acquisitions, development, and expansion.

External growth though, has some element of outside control factors, such as the economy in a given market. There are parts of the equation, however, that a REIT executive can control, most notably the risk he or she is willing to take. For example, when looking at a particular acquisition opportunity, a REIT operator has all of the information he or she needs to make the deal, such as some of the analytical studies mentioned in the first part of this chapter.

The control factor comes in making the right call and in taking the right risks.

Acquisition opportunities, at least the good ones, have several other factors. One is a REIT's access to the capital markets and the cost of that capital. That in of itself can be a challenge, due to factors such as the REIT's balance sheet, the cap rate of the property and surrounding properties, interest rates, the supply-and-demand forces of the current market, and the location of the potential deal.

One example of a REIT sector that took advantage of buying opportunities in terms of improving its external growth factors was the apartment REITs of the early 1990s. Several apartment REITs were able to buy dozens of buildings at discounted rates coming off the late 1980s overbuilding phase. Many of the sellers were banks seeking to dump repossessed properties or were overextended developers.

One caveat to any buying opportunity is the cost of capital. This is not merely what it costs to loan money or what the interest rate is. Like in any other business deal, if the cost of capital exceeds what the projected profit will be, then the deal may not work out.

Cost of equity capital, for example, is broken down into several calculations. One is what is known as nominal, which means that a REIT's current earnings — its FFO or its AFFO — and its net assets must be allocated among a larger number of common shares. Another calculation is considered, the true or long-term cost of equity, which looks at dilution over a longer time and also puts a premium on what shareholders expect on their return for the invested capital.

The final element in studying a potential acquisition deal for a REIT is the REIT's FFO accretion, which is commonly referred to as the spread. This is the difference between what a REIT can earn on its invested capital and the cost to obtain that capital. The spread again brings the risk element in the equation: this time, the REIT executive needs to figure out how much of a spread he or she is willing to accept, weighed against other economic factors.

Acquisitions are not the only method a REIT can use to grow its FFO through external forces. A REIT can also develop new properties and expand on current ones. These methods, especially development, can be risky and time consuming and normally require demonstrated expertise. Finally, a REIT can form a joint venture with other companies, allowing it to go slower and share the risks. It can even invest in boutique-style loans, such as a mezzanine and bridge loans. The latter loans are more prominent in mortgage REITs than in equity REITs.

Proper Valuations

Clearly a REIT's FFO is the most prominent way of judging the value of a REIT. But it is not the only method.

One well-known method is called a net asset value analysis, the public real estate version of the replacement cost philosophy detailed earlier in the chapter. A REIT's net asset value refers to the commonly accepted market value of a company's assets and properties after subtracting its liabilities and obligations.

A net asset value lends itself well to a REIT because of a REIT's constantly changing property values. But to some in the REIT industry that can be a disadvantage because some investors hold the view that a REIT's market value is not only based on property assets, but also on the total business the company operates.

Another method of determining a REIT's value is what is known as earnings before interest, taxes, depreciation, and amortization. Well known in the investment community as EBITDA, this method measures cash flow composed of earnings before interest, taxes, depreciation, and amortization. For REIT purposes, the equation divides the total market cap of equity and the nominal value of company debt of the REIT by the total earnings before interest, taxes, depreciation, and amortization.

This process is helpful for investors seeking to compare REITs with varied amounts of leverage on the balance sheets.

Much of this chapter so far has focused on why a proper REIT valuation process requires calculations and methodologies that go past simple earnings per share analysis. Still, earnings per share should not be completely ignored.

For starters, earnings per share is the most popular method used by Wall Street analysts covering the thousands of publicly traded companies. It is so popular that an investor looking into a REIT should not totally ignore it, even if other methodologies carry more importance.

The trick is to not overly rely on the earnings per share analysis, even though many Wall Street analysts seem to do just that, as do some business news reporters.

One final and simple method of judging the value of a REIT lies in the dividend yield and the dividend coverage, also known as a payout ratio. A REIT's dividend yield tracks interest rate drops closely because when interest rates go down, it tends to make high-dividend yields a more sought-after investment.

Although all of these measurement tools, on an individual and collective basis, go a long way toward determining the true value of a REIT, it is also important and telling to see how REITs perform against other REITs and against the entire stock market.

Unfortunately, like many other big-picture questions on Wall

Street and in the investment world, there is not a concrete answer to that question. Researchers Su Han Chan, John Erickson, and Ko Wang looked into just that in their book *Real Estate Investment Trusts: Structure, Performance, and Investment Opportunities.*

The evidence is that there is not enough evidence to prove too much. "In summary," the authors wrote, "the evidence indicates that over the long run, portfolios of REITs have not outperformed the stock market."

But the authors add that during specific time periods they and other researchers have studied, some REITs have outperformed the market, while others have underperformed it. In many ways, that is much like Wall Street itself: a good long-term investment as proven by history but a rather unpredictable investment in the short term.

15

REITs and the Individual Investor

The rise of the stock market in the late 1990s did more than provide on-paper riches for thousands of investors. It also opened the door to myriad opportunities for individual investors to enter the stock market and, it follows, in REIT investing.

Moreover, new opportunities have arisen this past decade, especially considering advances in technology. In early 2008, the methods available for an individual to invest in REITs were akin to betting on the Super Bowl: there is the bet on the score of the actual game, and then there are dozens of other betting possibilities, from the songs played at a half-time show to the result of the pregame coin flip.

However, even though this chapter is dedicated to how an individual can take part in REIT investing, a good place to start is the role of institutions in REIT investing. This is because over the latter half of the past decade, the role of institutions investing in REITs has grown significantly, so much so that an examination of how they do it and how they are doing could be helpful to an individual investor.

The difference between an individual investor and institutional investor is that an institution is made up of individuals' money pooled together in an account for a larger group, such as mutual and pension funds. Meanwhile, a straight-up individual investor is someone who is buying and selling shares of stocks or other investments strictly for personal gain.

The street between institutional investors and REITs goes two ways, as both entities need each other. REITs that seek institutions are looking for advantages such as a lower cost of capital, less time spent on raising debt and equity capital, and more stability in share prices. Plus, a long-term relationship with a deep-pocketed institutional investor can only bolster a REIT's long-term outlook.

Institutional investors, on the other hand, get what individual investors do out of REITs, only on a much larger scale: access to real estate ownership through a less-risk partnership model and regular dividends.

There are six types of institutional investors that tend to migrate toward REITs, with mutual funds and state-based pension funds being two of the most prominent. With mutual funds, especially the bigger ones on the market, the time spent in one particular REIT is rather short, mostly no longer than a year. This is because of the rapid buy/sell processes most mutual funds must undertake to remain competitive. Mutual fund managers also sell off shares on a hastened schedule to maximize gains and minimize losses.

Pension funds tend to follow a similar trend line as mutual funds when it comes to investing in REITs, adding in a more long-term outlook into the equation. Pension funds are attracted to REITs because the investments offer a portfolio diversification option, in addition to a sound hedge against inflation.

Pension funds, much like REITs, are broken down into various sub-sections. A pension fund can be a public entity, such as a state employees' or public teachers' group. One of the more prominently known public pension funds is the California Public Employees' Retirement System, commonly known as CalPERS. Other pension funds that have invested in REITs include ones stemming from corporations, foundations, and endowments.

In addition to mutual and pension funds, there are a few other institutional investors that have raised their level of REIT holdings over the past five years. The list includes insurance companies, foreign investors, and real estate investment advisers. Members of the last group use their expertise in the real estate industry to try and find the right REIT investing formula.

The Individual

The individual investor might not have the same access to investment capital as a pension fund or an insurance company, but the opportunities are virtually the same, even if they are on a considerably lower financial scale. The first place an individual investor could look to find a particular REIT to invest in is within the REIT subsectors detailed in the second section of this book.

For some investors, however, those sectors might be too specific. Therefore, investors, analysts, and executives have created another section of REITs, where retail might mix with hotel and warehouse might mix with apartments. In his book *Investing in REITs*, now in its third edition, nationwide REIT expert and attorney Ralph Block breaks down the four possibilities investors have as follows: blue-chip REITs, growth REITs, value REITs, and so-called bond-proxy REITs.

There is no absolute formula for what would constitute a blue-chip REIT, although investors and advisers tend to agree that for a REIT to reach blue-chip status, there are a few must-haves. The list, not much different from what would be expected of a non-REIT blue-chip, includes attributes such as a strong balance sheet, highly thought-of and proven management, expertise in the given market, a growing dividend payout, and access to capital in both good and bad markets.

Blue-chip REITs also lose and gain blue-chip status from time to time, as a by-product of the constantly changing stock market. This was proven in 2007, as just about every publicly traded REIT suffered in some way as the subprime mortgage meltdown brought down the entire sector. Even REITs considered by some to be blue-chip stocks, such as New York-based Kimco Realty Corp. or Indianapolis-based Simon Property Group, struggled, share-value wise, in 2007.

However, blue-chip stocks, including REITs, get to that level for multiple reasons, and so it might be a good idea to include some in any REIT portfolio.

Not many REITs are considered to be growth stocks. The REIT investing world is not for those seeking fast-growth stocks such as technology or pharmaceutical companies.

Furthermore, by the nature of the business REITs are in and by the nature of the tax laws that govern the sector, REITs do not tend to grow rapidly, and they also do not have large sums of money for reinvesting in the business, as 90 percent of the cash flow gets returned to investors in the form of dividend.

Nonetheless, REIT growth stocks do exist. One example of a growth REIT stock is a company that grows its funds from operations (FFO) at a rate faster than 4 to 6 percent, what has been considered the industry average for the past few years.

Because the REIT market has essentially created space for blue-chip and growth REITs, it follows that there is also a spot for value REITs. A value stock is one an investor buys because he or she thinks its value has gone unappreciated in some way and is a bargain at its current price. Just like in the entire stock market, a value REIT can be a company with management turnover, for example, or some previous balance sheet problems it has corrected.

One final REIT stock in this investor category of choices is what Block refers to as the bond-proxy REIT. REITs that fall under this category, according to Block, have little growth within FFO or dividends but instead focus on maintaining low debt levels and consistent property holdings. In this way, the REIT performs like a less risky, more reliable bond.

Those categories, in addition to the previously mentioned REIT subsectors, only go as far as pointing out the types of REITs an individual can invest in. As far as investing strategies, there are five popular methods an individual investor can use to invest in a REIT, including:

Real Estate Mutual Funds

There are almost 100 mutual funds available to the individual investor that focus on real estate investing. Furthermore, a small amount of those mutual funds have a hyper-focus on REITs. Just like a large-scale mutual fund, these focused mutual funds are drawn to REITs because of the high dividend yields.

Of course, that same attraction is one of the negative aspects an individual investor faces by choosing the mutual fund option. That is, the investor will not be eligible to receive the dividend, as he or she would not have direct ownership of the stock.

On the positive side, though, choosing a mutual fund to invest in REITs allows the risk of the investment to be mitigated by the mutual fund, which could have hundreds of other stocks in its portfolio. Also, a mutual fund has a professionally licensed management team, and although that does not mean it will be mistake free, it does bring some past experience to the investment.

Real estate unit investment trusts could be considered mutual fund light. This is because a unit investment trust, or a UIT, is not actively managed like a mutual fund is. Instead, it has a predetermined existence, set up primarily so it can trade shares on a secondary market, much like a closed-end mutual fund.

A positive feature of a UIT is that its closed structure sometimes provides a buying opportunity for investors to get shares at prices lower than what a REIT might be going for on the open market. Investing in a UIT also has positive tax benefits for the individual investor.

Nonetheless, this investment choice has some negatives for an individual investor, most notably a lack of control over investment choices. That is true in a mutual fund, too, but in that investment the managers and stock pickers are being trusted to do a good job. Because a UIT is set up with a passive management structure, the result is that there is little chance of changing the investments due to market conditions.

Exchange traded funds: The investing concept known as exchange traded funds was the Next Big Thing when it hit Wall Street in the early 2000s. By 2008, the concept, which revolves around the idea that an investor can buy shares of an entire index of stocks, as opposed to just one or two stocks in the index, had indeed become so popular that companies had been formed to sell just ETFs.

An ETF, essentially, is set up to represent all the stocks of a certain index, be it utility companies or REITs. An ETF is just like a normal stock in that an investor can sell and trade ETF shares just like shares of a particular company, and the value of an ETF goes up and down throughout the day, too.

One advantage of buying ETFs with a REIT focus as opposed to investing in REIT-based mutual funds is that with ETFs, the individual investor can have a bigger say in buy-and-sell calls, as there is no middle-man mutual fund manager in the way. The disadvantage is that ETFs are bought and sold through a stock broker or another third party; thus, there could be commissions and other fees.

Outright Ownership

This is the most obvious, yet most daunting, way of entering the REIT market; there is no cushion, like there might be with mutual funds, UITs, or even ETFs, which by the nature of their existence are diversified entities. Therefore, financial planners and advisers recommend that an individual investor buying shares of REITs on his own create a baseline of diversity by buying at least seven different REITs, which should come from multiple REIT sectors.

The advantages of buying a REIT's shares outright, as opposed to doing it through mutual funds or some other investment portfolio are fairly obvious: the investor gets a complete share of the rewards, including the dividends, tax benefits, and any increase in the stock price. The negatives, however, are fairly obvious too: total control also means that the investor has total risk. Unlike a mutual fund manager or an ETF adviser, an individual investor is not investing other people's money.

Before deciding on a particular strategy, or which parts of those strategies to combine together when investing in REITs, there are several other points to consider. These are especially true for an investor going the outright ownership route but are also relevant to any strategy.

For example, investing in publicly traded REITs that are fully integrated, self-administered, and self-managed is a key principle, according to many financial advisers and money planners. This goes a long way toward ensuring that the executives at the top of the REIT are running a solid organization.

A fully integrated REIT is one where the REIT management or other internal personnel are fully responsible for handling all real estate services, from acquisition of properties to construction to renovation projects to leasing and property sale issues. In a similar fashion, a self-administered and self-managed REIT is one where the REIT executives and operators administer and manage all aspects of the company, as opposed to contracting services out to another firm.

Researching the management of a REIT is another integral component to REIT investment selection. In this way, REIT investing is much like Wall Street investing, in that many individual investors will follow managers and executives who go from company to company, as opposed to buying or selling simply on the merits of that business.

In REITs, investors tend to look for two positive attributes in a management team. One is the real estate experience the executives bring to the company. This is important because the real estate industry, as proven through time, is cyclical. As such, investors are seeking a company with an executive management team that has a "been-there, done-that" approach in the face of a difficult market.

Another aspect investors look for in a REIT management team is the level of insider ownership, or how many shares of the company each executive holds and when he or she bought them (or sold them). Although this information is relatively easy to find by going to the company's Securities and Exchange Commission filings, it is somewhat harder to judge its actual value when making an investment choice.

Logically, it would hold that if executives have a large stake in the company they work for, then they will work harder and do more to see that the company does well. In many cases, today's publicly traded REITs were once privately held companies with the same management team, so a personal investment could run deep.

However, there have been several studies published on how stocks with high levels of insider ownership perform, and there is not much of a consensus in the investing community on the issue. Although it looks good on paper, there is no long-term scientific proof that insider ownership leads to a better stock performance or a higher dividend payout.

There are also a few macro-economic points to consider when choosing a REIT-investing strategy.

For instance, the current interest rate environment could be the difference between an average-performing REIT and one that is exceeding expectations. The higher the interest rates go, the less attractive high-yield stocks like REITs become. This is because the rising interest rate could both negatively affect the REIT's real estate operations and its share price.

But some recent investment studies have shown that the interest rate factor is sometimes given too much emphasis by investors. Some in the REIT investing community say another source for looking at how REITs will perform is the correlation coefficient.

As mentioned in Chapter 1, correlations that compare one asset class to another to predict what each class will do over time are a standard measuring tool in the money-managing and financial-planning community. The correlation measurement ranges from a full -1, where the classes will do the complete opposite of each other to a full +1, where the classes will be completely in sync with each other. The lower the correlation between two asset classes, the lower the volatility of the entire portfolio. That low correlation, in turn, increases the return rates of the entire portfolio.

REITs tend to have a low correlation. For instance, in one major study, the National Association of Real Estate Investment Trusts (NAREIT) reported that the correlation of REIT returns with other investments has declined over the last 30 years. From 1994 to 2004, the association reported, REIT stocks had a .028 correlation when compared against the S&P 500 Index. Therefore, REIT fluctuations had only a 28 percent correlation with the S&P's heavily tracked index.

That number is lower than just about any other sector on the stock market, another piece of information for investors to consider when deciding how to be involved in the REIT market.

CASE STUDY: ADAM PARISH

Individual Investor

www.reitmedia.com

Celebration, Florida

Adam Parish has been investing in REITs since 2002, when he bought shares in Duke Realty Corp. Since then, he has bought and sold shares of several other REITs, and he has even bought shares of Duke Realty (DRE) again, as recently as early 2008.

"The stock is down big, and I think they are making great long-term developments that are perceived as expensive in the short term," said Parish of his January 2008 purchase of shares of Duke. "I think it should rebound, and my initial investment yield will be almost 8 percent."

CASE STUDY: ADAM PARISH

Parish also owned shares of Trustreet Properties, Inc. and BNP Residential before both of those companies were acquired by private equity firms in 2007, which Parish says paid off well; Trustreet was bought by GE Capital in 2007, while BNP was bought by an Australian private equity firm.

Parish, who also runs a REIT blog and Web site at **www.reitmedia. com**, was initially attracted to the REIT industry for the reasons the industry was set up in the first place: access. "The best part about publicly traded REITs is that anyone with a few hundred dollars can be in an industry that was once limited to the ultra-rich," Parish said.

"It is a great sense of patriotism and ownership, as real estate is all around us. Many of us work, shop, eat, or even sleep in buildings owned by REITs, which means it could be owned, in part, by the person standing next to you at the checkout or the person sipping coffee at the table next to you."

Still, nothing is perfect in the world of REIT investing. "Probably the biggest challenge," Parish said, "is the mountain of paperwork created by public REITs and parsing through financial statements."

Getting Going

An examination of the types of REITs and the types of investing available in the REIT market is only about 70 percent of the entire REIT investing equation. Before entering the REIT market, or before making any investment decisions, an investor should have a plan. It is the type of plan most commonly discussed with a financial planner, a money manager, or sometimes even an accountant.

The plan revolves around a series of psychological-type

queries designed to answer the one true key question: what is your pain tolerance for possibly losing money? Therefore, before investing in any REITs it makes sense to know the answers to the following questions: how dependent on the source of the investing money are you to live; how aggressive are you willing to be, or how tepid of an investor are you; and how do you and the people close to you emotionally handle financial losses?

The answers to those questions go a long way toward determining where an institutional investor will be on the next phase of investing in REITs: asset allocation.

There are two steps to the asset allocation process in the REIT investing sector. One part is figuring out what types of REITs to invest in, how many, and how much of each to hold. In addition you must decide on an investment approach, choosing from possibilities such as outright ownership, mutual funds, and ETFs. A large portion of this book has been spent providing a guide to that part of the equation.

The next part is to determine how much space REITs should take up in an investment portfolio, next to other stocks, bonds, mutual funds, and any other type of investment vehicle. An entire industry, that of financial planning, has been created over the last 25 years to help individual investors figure this out.

The industry relies on what is known as modern portfolio theory, which is the concept that when a broad mix of investments, such as stocks, treasury bonds, and even REITs, are mixed together in one portfolio, the risk will go down, and the returns will go up over time. In that way, the modern portfolio theory is similar to a mutual fund, which is designed to mitigate risk while maximizing returns.

There is little consensus in the financial planning community as to how many REITs an individual investor should own while using the modern portfolio theory. Some of the answer depends on how the investor feels toward risk, and other parts of the answer depends on how much money the investor has to invest. Although investing in REITs is not necessarily reserved for the wealthy, it always helps to have a cushion to absorb some of the losses.

It might seem daunting for an individual investor to get going on his or her own in investing in REITs, but there is plenty of help, especially considering the proliferation of investing-based Web sites over the last five years.

For research purposes, an individual investor can start with probing the history of the indexes set up to monitor the REIT industry. An index computes the average stock price out of a given list of stocks, which can help an investor monitor how a particular market is faring on a given day or a time period. Wall Street is full of indexes, from the Dow Jones Industrial Average to the S&P 500 to the family of Russell indexes.

There is no shortage of indexes covering the REIT industry, either. Some of the more prominent ones include the Dow Jones Equity All REIT Total Return Index, which includes all of the publicly traded REITs in the United States on a continuing basis; the NAREIT Index, similar to the Dow Jones model, only it is monitored by the REIT industry's trade association and is rebalanced monthly to allow for changes in the marketplace; the NAREIT Equity Index, which is the same as the previous index, only without mortgage REITs; and the NAREIT 50 Index, a compilation of the 50 largest publicly traded REITs.

Several financial services firms and investment research companies have created other, more micro-specific, REIT indexes in recent years. A popular one in individual investor circles over the past year is the Morgan Stanley REIT Index, which is made up of REITs that meet certain minimum requirements, such as a predetermined baseline market share, trading volume, and market capitalization. The index, which is under the ticker symbol RMZ on the American Stock Exchange, covers only REITs with at least a six-month trading history on a major stock exchange, and it does not track healthcare or mortgage REITs.

Two other established REIT indexes are the S&P REIT Composite Index, which monitors the share prices of 100 REITs, including mortgage REITs, and the Wilshire Real Estate Securities Index, which tracks REITs and other real estate-related companies, such as homebuilders, developers, and hotel operators.

Although indexes are useful tools for investors attempting to see how a certain part of the REIT market has been performing, it is only one tool of several that financial advisers suggest when investing in REITs.

Another source of information is the Internet, with the caveat that like anything else in cyberspace, there is the potential for both misinformation and information overload. But some good places to start would be a REIT's own Web site, which can be found by searching the database on National Association of Real Estate Investment Trust's Web site, **www. nareit.com**.

Although a company's own Web site has some obvious bias built in, it can be helpful to get a baseline of what the company's strategy is and how it plans to go about executing that strategy. A company Web site will also list key management and executives.

Other Web sites that could prove useful to individual investors researching particular REITs are Google Finance and Yahoo! Finance. Those sites are just two of many that have set up detailed profiles of every publicly traded company. The profiles include data such as historical prices, insider ownership levels, and earnings information. The profiles also include links to the REIT's quarterly and annual SEC filings, which is another source of information.

Although company Web sites and the search portals such as Google and Yahoo! provide free research, there are dozens of pay-research options that offer a more detailed and thorough analysis. Those include services from brokerage companies, such as Morgan Stanley and Merrill Lynch, in addition to private research firms, such as SNL Financial.

There are even more sources of information for the individual investor, ones that are not necessarily on the Internet. Those include newsletters such as and *The Essential REIT*, published by Ralph Block, the previously mentioned renowned REIT expert, and *Realty Stock Review*, another California-based publication covering the industry.

Other sources of current information on the REIT industry can come from daily newspapers and weekly magazines, such as *The Wall Street Journal* and *Business Week*. The REIT industry has become so popular over the past few years that some of the more established publications have even assigned one reporter to cover strictly REITs.

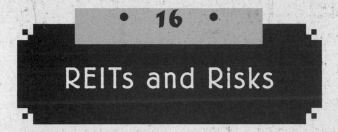

16

REITs and Risks

Although the question of risk and how much of it an individual investor is willing to take on can be sufficiently answered only by that specific investor, there is another side of risk within REIT investing.

There are two sides to this larger risk equation, both relevant to how an individual investor approaches the REIT market. As with just about any other segment of the stock market, there are some risks that are specific to each REIT, while other risks are pertinent to an entire REIT sector or even the entire REIT industry.

Of course, when dealing with any publicly traded company, there is the infamous Wall Street guilt-by-association syndrome. This is when an entire sector suffers when problems are isolated within one or two companies. From Enron on down, there are dozens of examples of companies' stock being battered by Wall Street, just for essentially being part of a sector with an underperforming or problematic company. This happens in REITs, too.

But specifically within individual REITs, investors should be aware of a multitude of risks that go past the simple daily ups and downs of the company's shares and the guilt-by-association effect. These potential problems include:

- **Management issues:** Even good executives make bad calls. On the flip side, bad managers sometimes make good calls. The trick is to recognize the difference and then be sure to stay with the companies that are run by managers you believe in.

A bad executive management team can cause a litany of problems within a REIT, which in turn could have an adverse effect on the REIT's share price and its dividend yield. These problems, all of which have happened in one form or another to various REITs over the past few years, include overestimating and overreaching on future FFO projections; expanding too rapidly and taking on too much debt in the process; going into new markets, sectors, and geographies without conducting adequate research first; and overpaying for properties and then having to sell some or all of them at a loss.

A management team that tends to avoid those missteps over the years can develop a good reputation and following in the industry.

Therein lies another problem REITs might face: replacing a quality executive who retires or moves on to another organization or phase in life. This is especially pertinent with smaller REITs that do not have the financial resources some of the bigger firms do.

- **Financial issues:** High debt levels within in a REIT are a good sign that the REIT is spending money and as such is growing its funds from operations (FFO). But too much debt, especially too much short-term debt, can wreck a REIT's balance sheet.

Furthermore, a REIT that takes on too much debt also hinders its ability to get new financing and complete other acquisitions.

- **Size issues:** Even the biggest REITs, from a market capitalization perspective, are small by Wall Street big-company standards. Although the basic business theory that a smaller company is more nimble than a bigger one and thus can make decisions quicker is true to a large extent, small could still leave a company gasping. For example, costs that all companies must incur, such as such as the fees associated with Sarbanes-Oxley or a marketing budget, mean more to a smaller firm than a big firm.

- **Local issues:** This is the dark side that can be occasionally found when REITs focus on one geographical area, like some diversified REITs do.

The issues can be of the big-problem variety, such as the case in Southwest Florida in 2004 and 2005, when a succession of hurricanes battered the state and caused billions of dollars of damage to thousands of commercial and residential properties, some of which were owned by REITs. On a smaller, less destructive scale, problems can arise in certain markets that are struggling financially. For example, a retail REIT focusing on malls in the Northeast United States or an industrial REIT focusing on buildings in the Pacific Northwest can run into problems if those specific markets experience a recession-like atmosphere.

- **Trend issues:** This last potential issue individual investors should be aware of when investing in REITs is one of the hardest to figure out. This is because it is all about predicting trends and which business concepts are moneymakers and which ones are fads.

For instance, take the concept of New Urbanism in building and development, which follows the sustainable theory of building housing communities together with places where people can also work and play. An investor thinking of buying shares in a REIT that is undertaking a New Urbanism strategy needs to be able to project the long-term success of the concept, not just the REIT.

In addition to those problems that could affect individual REITs, there are also several issues that could matter to entire REIT sectors, even to all REITs. Some of those potential problems have been covered in various chapters in this book, such as the impact of rising interest rates and the market forces of supply-and-demand issues.

Another potential problem that could affect all REITs, loosely related to supply-and-demand issues, is the problem of overbuilding. This is exactly what happened in the latter half of 2007, when the nation's residential housing industry began to collapse due, in part, to a massive overbuilding phase earlier in the decade. The housing issues set off other problems, such as the subprime mortgage crisis, and by the end of the year, just about every publicly traded REIT had lost some of its market capitalization.

One final issue that lingers as a potential risk for all REITs is that of REITs' own existence. Although there is no reason or evidence to think the legal structure set up to oversee REITs is in jeopardy of collapsing, the possibility exists that parts of that structure could change, given that REITs are a government creation, born in 1960 out of a desire to give the common man a chance to own a piece of several real estate properties.

Trend Lines

Most REIT observers predict that if and when the federal government makes any changes to the REIT governing structure, they will most likely be minor. The system has been working for almost 50 years, REIT observers and analysts say, and there is no reason to abandon that strategy now. Also, a few recent structural changes, such as the REIT Modernization Act of 1999, addressed many of the issues concerning investors and REIT operators.

Still, there are several other non-government related issues and trends that are likely to have a big impact on the REIT industry over the newt few years. Although these issues are not risky in of themselves, looking into them could provide some clarity to the future of the industry.

It looked as 2008 would be a good baseline to monitor some of these trends. Many REIT observers pegged this year to be a watershed one for REITs because the previous year was the first time in nearly a decade the industry had negative returns. Indeed, the entire REIT industry produced a -15.60 percent return in 2007 after providing an average annual return of 23 percent from 1999 to 2006, according to the National Association of Real Estate Investment Trusts (NAREIT).

Therefore, investors and analysts want to see how the industry and individual REITs adjust to the changes in the marketplace. Some of the trends to watch for in the REIT industry over the next few years include:

- **Other services:** Most equity REITs provide customers with only on product — space, be it space to live in, work in, shop in, or vacation in. But over the last year or two, some REIT executives have begun to realize that those customers have other needs that a REIT might be able to provide for.

For instance, some apartment REITs have begun contracting with high-speed Internet providers to bring connections to the apartment residents. This is what the industry refers to as a value-added component, one a REIT can charge a premium for. Other apartment REITs have expanded that line of thinking even further, setting up online rent paying, maintenance, and accounting services.

There is even more potential for new businesses REITs can get into, such as property development and commercial banking.

Of course, expanding into new business lines has two clear risks: first, the REIT needs to monitor its customer base and income stream, to make sure it is still a REIT, not a diversified real estate company. Second, going into new business, although potentially lucrative, can also dilute the REIT's brand and focus. Some investors buy into REITs because of what they are already doing, not what they are not.

- **Going global:** The concept that business has gone global is nothing new, but REITs have been slow to join the international parade. Some REITs, especially industrial and warehouse REITs, have been putting global expansion on high priority the past few years, especially as the market slump lingers stateside.

There are several advantages a domestic REIT can capitalize on when doing business abroad. One is price points. Many times, European and Asian property markets work at opposite cycles as some in the United States, which could lead to buying opportunities. Another positive attribute of investing in global properties is that it could ultimately expand a REIT's domestic client base, by getting connected with other like-minded international customers. A third advantage is that the United States REIT market is one of the most advanced in the world, and an experienced REIT manager can use that experience to his or her advantage overseas.

Just as with expanding into other business, expanding globally is not without its risks. First and foremost are exchange-rate issues. While in 2008, with the value of the American dollar being battered around abroad that would be a plus, not a negative, an experienced and savvy investor knows those valuations can, and likely will, change. Another risk REITs face in investing abroad is language and culture barriers, issues any global business faces. A third, more micro issue REITs could be dealing with by expanding globally is taxes. That is, any income a REIT earns in a foreign country will be subject to that country's tax laws, not the ones that govern REITs in the United States.

- **Technology advances:** For reasons industry observers and experts have struggled to understand, REITs have been one of the slowest industries to accept and use the power of the Internet. One of the biggest complaints from the individual investment community about REITs is that the Web sites tend to be boring or one-dimensional.

But that could be on the cusp of change. For instance, Anatole Pevnev, a 20-year REIT research industry veteran, has seen his Web-based REIT podcast service explode in popularity since he debuted it in 2005. The site, **www.reitcafe.com**, offers weekly downloads of podcasts that contain interviews with REIT executives.

In the site's first month alone, it received more than 112,000 hits from visitors in nearly 50 countries. By early 2008, Pevnev reported that the interviews and other podcasts, such as company conference calls, were so popular that other REIT analysts and investors were listening to them in their cars or on the train to and from work.

Actual REITs are slowly following the lead of the investment community. In 2006 and 2007, several REITs invested time and money in renovating Web sites, while others began using the Internet more often for purchasing, accounting, and other services.

Finally, in a strong sign that a technological revolution is underway in the industry, many REIT executives have told shareholders and investors that the future vitality of the industry will require an improved technology infrastructure, another way of saying companies will be spending more money on technology in the near future.

- **Merger activity:** When a private equity firm buys a publicly traded company, many times the latter's shareholders rejoice because it allows them to cash out of their investment with what they hope is a premium sales price. REIT investors, however, sometimes lament the sale of a REIT to a private equity firm because it puts their dividend at risk, as the new version of the company might no longer be subject to REIT rules and standards.

It is for that reason that investors should be cognizant of the trend lines in the private equity buyout market.

During 2006 and most of 2007, Wall Street private equity firms were flush with cash and were using many of those funds to take public companies private, including businesses such as Outback Steakhouse and Chrysler. Several REITs took the private equity-buying binge as an opportunity to cash out and go private, too.

Between 2006 and the first half of 2007, there were 23 mergers and acquisitions involving REITs, worth more than $106 billion, according to research firm SNL Financial. This trend seemed to end almost as quickly as it began, though, because by the last quarter of 2007 and into early 2008, there was little merger and acquisition activity in the REIT industry.

The rise and fall of the trend can be traced to the same reason: the nation's economic outlook. In 2005, when the housing market was peaking all over the country, from Miami to Minneapolis, lenders and banks were eager to lend money to private equity firms. But when the housing market started to crumble, followed by the subprime mortgage problems and a fall in the stock market, many of those same lenders moved on to other opportunities.

Although most analysts predict the private equity buyout market will be at a standstill in 2008 and several years thereafter, there are still some buyout trends to watch for. For example, some analysts are predicting that the highly leveraged private equity firms that are no longer in the merger and acquisition game will be replaced by entities that rely less on debt, such as foreign investors and pension funds.

- **Activist investors:** Individual REITs have been able to avoid the wrath of activist investors for most of the last decade because the REIT industry has spent most of that time outperforming the market. That makes sense, since activist investors, a group made up mostly of hedge fund and mutual fund managers, focus all of their time and energy on underperforming companies.

For most of 2007, activist investors called for change in the structure, executive compensation, and business models of companies from newspaper holding operations to clothing retailers to homebuilders, all of which were suffering in one way or another. Individual REITs, for the most part, were off the list.

But the 2007 sell-off of REIT stocks jeopardizes the industry's position and makes the issue a trend worth monitoring. For example, in early 2008 the chief executive officer of ROCA Real Estate Securities, a Newport Beach, California-based private investment fund, wrote letters to a trio of REITs, according to a *Wall Street Journal* article. The letters, sent to executives at Glimcher Realty Trust, Cedar Shopping Centers, Inc., and One Liberty Properties, Inc., call for the retail REITs to either sell any low-quality malls to raise money to pay back debt or outright seek a buyout offer, the article said.

The outcome of that particular activist investor letter request, although important for the shareholders of those companies, might not be, and probably should not be, crucial to every individual REIT investor. It is worth monitoring though, because the market might breed more activist investors over the next few years.

- **Joint ventures:** A REIT that takes part in a joint venture in some ways is engaging in something similar to entering new business lines. The big difference with a joint venture is that this time a REIT shares some of the risks, and potential profits, with a non-REIT entity.

A joint venture is a partnership with an outside investor on a variety of projects, such as buying a single or a series of commercial properties, developing new projects, and consulting on other deals. The non-REIT partner tends to be a bank, a commercial lender, a pension fund, or some other institutional investor. The REIT brings the management, experience, and contacts to the partnership, while the non-REIT entity brings the money.

By some analysts' count, a successfully executed joint venture, at least when it comes to building acquisitions, is good for a 5 or 6 percent boost over the returns from a non-joint venture purchase.

It is no surprise then, that joint ventures turned into a growing trend in 2007, as REIT investors continued seeking new revenue sources. According to research firm SNL financial, there were more than 30 joint venture transactions involving a REIT in 2007, up from 13 in 2002.

Although those statistics show this trend is clearly worth

watching, it is also one that could be on the downswing due to the struggling economy. Some analysts were projecting that the joint venture trend might go into hibernation for some of the next few years, as REITs become more conservative with outside investments.

Coming Soon

Researching trends and knowing the risks is important in REIT investing, as it is in any type of investing, from low-risk treasury bonds to high-risk foreign stocks. But there is one question that nearly no amount of research can provide a clear-cut answer to: how much will REIT stocks grow?

A majority of the industry's observers, analysts and investors think REITs, both as a sector and as individual companies, will grow significantly over the next ten years.

That group has plenty of statistics to back that up, starting with the sector's run up in share prices over the eight-year period ending in 2007. Beyond that, the REIT industry has much room to grow, as only about 15 percent of the country's $11 trillion in real estate is currently owned by a REIT.

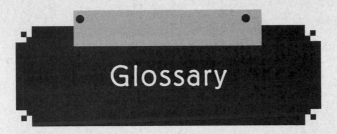

Glossary

Adjusted funds from operations (AFFO): A measurement of a real estate company's cash flow generated by operations. The first part of the calculation subtracts the REIT's funds from operations from normalized recurring expenditures that are capitalized by the REIT and then amortized but which are necessary to maintain a REIT's properties and its revenue stream. That includes items such as new carpeting in apartment units and leasing expenses. The second facet for calculating AFFO is to subtract what is known as the straight-lining of rents from the FFO. A REIT's AFFO is also known as cash available for distribution (CAD).

Amortization: The liquidation of debt using periodic payments of principle.

Apartments and multifamily housing: Apartment buildings are residential structures composed of five or more units in a single building or a series of buildings. Multifamily housing is used to describe of four or fewer residential units.

Blind pool: A commingled real estate fund that will bring in investment capital without going through an analysis of property assets.

Book value: The net value of a company's assets minus its liabilities, shown on its balance sheet through GAAP (see: generally accepted accounting principles). A company's book value will also reflect amortization and depreciation, which are expensed for accounting purposes.

C-Corporation: The Internal Revenue Service code for a corporation that forms under Subchapter C provisions. This entity, commonly referred to as a C-Corp, can be either publicly or privately held and is required to pay taxes on its net taxable income. Its shareholders also must pay income tax on any dividends.

Capital gains: The net proceeds from the resale of a capital item that exceed the book value of the asset.

Capitalization rates: A method of determining a commercial real estate property's risk level. A cap rate is determined by dividing a property's post-expenses net operating income by its purchase price. The higher the cap rate, the higher the return potential as well as the risk. The lower the cap rate, the lower the perceived risk. So, a property with an annual net operating income of $100,000 and an asking price of $1 million would have a 10 percent cap rate.

Cash or funds available for distribution (CAD or FAD): A REIT's ability to generate cash and to distribute dividends to its shareholders. This measurement is derived by subtracting nonrecurring expenditures from a REIT's FFO, on top of subtracting normalized recurring real estate-related expenditures and other non-cash items.

Cash yield on cost (CYC): A company's net operating income or its operating property revenues minus operating expenses.

When used properly, it is a good measurement of a company's return on assets or the money it has invested in a given property.

Collateralized mortgage obligations (CMOs): Real estate mortgages that are put together and sold in the form of various participating interests.

Credit tenant: A tenant with the size and financial strength worthy enough of being rated as an investment grade by one of three major credit agencies: Fitch, Moody's, or Standard & Poor's. An investment grade rating is seen as a good sign that the tenant will be able to pay rent, even in economic downturns or specific market slumps.

Debt capital: The amount of debt a REIT carries on a balance sheet, excluding equity capital, such as a common or preferred stock. This can include short-term variable-rate debt; secured or unsecured debt; and long-term, fixed-rate mortgage debt.

Depreciation: The decrease or loss in a property's value due to wear and tear, age, and other factors. Depreciation in accounting is a systematic allowance made for this loss, real or implied.

Discounted cash flow (DCF): A measurement designed to find the value of a REIT by calculating the current value of future distributable income. By looking at this measurement in conjunction with a REIT's net present value per share, investors can gauge whether the current share price is undervaluing or overvaluing a REIT.

Dividend reinvestment programs (DRiP): A program allowing REITs to directly offer an investor the opportunity to pass the quarterly dividend back to the company. The investment refund from the dividends can then be used for price appreciation and compounding without incurring brokerage fees. DRiPs allow investors to take advantage of dollar cost averaging with income — the corporate dividends — the company is paying out. This way, an investor gets the return of the yield as well as the potential of stock gains. An investor must still pay taxes on a DRiP.

DownREIT: A REIT that owns and operates properties other than its interest in a separate controlled partnership. This is similar to an UPREIT (see: umbrella partnership) with the main difference being that a downREIT is normally formed after the REIT has become a public entity.

EBITDA: Earnings before interest, taxes, depreciation, and amortization. Sometimes referred to as net operating income (see: net operating income).

Equitization: This process of how a tangible asset, such as real estate, is divided up among several investors and placed into publicly traded stock. In some accounting principles, it also allows the parent company of the entity to calculate the net income of subsidiaries on a monthly basis and then increase the investment, if necessary, before consolidating properties and assets.

Equity REIT: A REIT that owns or has a financial and/or equity interest in a variety of real estate.

Funds from operations (FFO): The net income a REIT generates, excluding gains or losses from sales of property and adding back real estate depreciation. When compared to normal corporate accounting, it is a good approximation of cash flow and considered to be an even better judge of operations than generally accepted accounting principles, the standard for American public companies.

Generally accepted accounting principles (GAAP): The method by which all publicly traded companies report financial numbers.

Hybrid REIT: A REIT that combines the investment strategies of both equity REITs and mortgage REITs.

Implied equity market cap: The market value of all outstanding common stock of a company when added to the value of all UPREIT partnership units, assuming those units were part of the REIT's stock. This measurement excludes convertible preferred stock, convertible debentures, and warrants.

Internal rate of return (IRR): This measurement allows an investor to calculate a total return, incorporating both the return on investment and the return of an investment into the equation. It is used to determine the percentage rate of return of all future cash receipts balanced against all cash contributions so that when each receipt and cash contribution is discounted to net present value, the sum is equal to zero when added together. This is a popular way of measuring a total return on an investment.

Leverage: The amount of debt in relation to either equity capital or total capital. In real estate, more leverage means both a greater risk and a greater potential payoff. If an investment carries a high margin or leverage, it holds that it will carry higher risk, as even a small decline in the asset's value will wreak havoc on the entire investment.

Liquidity: The ability to convert assets into cash without an appreciable loss in value. A higher liquidity signifies it will be an easy conversion, while a lower liquidity signifies it will be a more difficult transition.

Loan to value (LTV): The proportion of borrowings to real estate or total assets. A lower value normally indicates lower risk.

Mortgage REIT: A REIT that makes or owns loans and other obligations that are secured by real estate collateral. This term also refers to REITs that lend money in non-mortgage transactions, such as a mezzanine or a bridge loan.

Net asset value (NAV): The commonly accepted market value of a company's assets and properties after subtracting its liabilities and obligations. This measurement tool, although popular for many REIT investors, is not fully comprehensive because it relies only on property assets.

Net income: The profits a business earns after expenses are subtracted from revenues. Real estate depreciation is considered an expense under generally accepted accounting principles (GAAP).

Positive spread investing (PSI): A common way for a public company to manage its risk while simultaneously earning a rate of return that exceeds its capital costs. For a REIT, PSI involves the ability to raise funds (both equity and debt) at a cost significantly less than the initial returns that can be obtained on real estate transactions. The contribution of funds to generate the PSI normally comes from three areas: investment yield, capital costs, and rate of activity.

Price-to-earnings ratios (P/E ratio): The measurement between a company's earnings per share and its stock price. It is calculated by dividing the stock price by the company's earnings per share, on either a trailing 12-month basis or a forward-looking basis.

Real estate investment trust (REIT): A REIT is a company that owns and operates income-producing real estate, including office buildings, hotels, apartments, medical office parks, and even, occasionally, golf courses. Other REITs, ones known as mortgage REITs, stick strictly to financing other real estate deals and projects. To qualify as a REIT under the federal guidelines, the company must distribute at least 90 percent of its taxable income to shareholders annually through dividends.

Real Estate Investment Trust Act of 1960: The federal law that gave birth to REITs. The original goal, which carries through today in many ways, was to allow small investors the ability to pool their investments in real estate so that they could get the same benefits as if they directly owned the property. The REIT allows those investors to diversify their risks. REITs have to follow certain tax and dividend guidelines, otherwise the company is forced to suspend or outright relinquish its REIT status.

REIT Modernization Act of 1999: One of several important changes to the original REIT legislation. It allows a REIT to own up to 100 percent of a taxable REIT subsidiary that can provide services to REIT tenants and others, a change that allows a REIT to save on expenses and operate more efficiently. The law also changed the minimum distribution requirement from 95 percent to 90 percent of a REIT's taxable income, a number consistent with the REIT rules on the books from 1960 to 1980.

Sale-leaseback: A process where a seller deeds property to a buyer for some type of consideration, financial or otherwise, and the buyer simultaneously leases the property back to the seller.

Securitization: The process of financing a pool of similar but unrelated financial assets by issuing investors stock for claims against the cash flow and other economic benefits generated by the pool of assets.

Specialty REIT: A REIT that owns or lends money to a type of property outside the realm of a normal REIT. A specialty REIT can own properties such as a movie theater, a timber company that owns large swaths of land, a golf course, or a race car track.

Standard deviation: A key measurement of risk and volatility in any portfolio. A portfolio with a low standard deviation helps bring down the risk but also provides lower returns.

Straight-lining: A calculation derived from the average of a tenant's rent payments over the entire lifetime of the lease. This measurement is a generally accepted accounting principles requirement for REITs.

Tax Reform Act of 1986: A federal law that allowed REITs to operate and manage most types of income-producing commercial properties, as opposed to just straight-up ownership. The law is considered one of the more significant pieces of REIT legislation.

Tenant in common: A structured deal that allows individual investors to pool their money to buy commercial properties and other large real estate holdings, leaving the management of the actual building to another entity. Also known as a 1031 exchange.

Triple net: A type of lease where the tenant is required to pay a predetermined amount of a given property's recurring maintenance and operating costs. These can include insurance, property taxes, and utilities.

Umbrella partnership REIT (UPREIT): This is an operating partnership where the partners of one REIT team up with the principles of another, newer REIT. For their respective interests in the operating partnership, the partners from the older REIT contribute the properties, while the new REIT contributes the cash proceeds from its public offering. After a given time, often one year, the partners are allowed to have the same liquidity of the REIT shareholders by selling their pieces of their partnership for either cash or REIT shares. Also, when a partner in this partnership holds the units until death, the federal estate tax allow the beneficiaries to sell the units for cash or REIT shares without paying income taxes.

Volatility: The fluctuation of a stock price, from day to day, or sometimes, from hour to hour. Volatility is a key factor investors look at when deciding if, and how much, to invest in a REIT.

Weighted average cost of capital (WACC): The weighted average of a REIT's debt and equity costs. This is important for investors because if a company's WACC projects a positive cash flow looking ahead, that is a good sign for a good investment. If the projections are negative, then the investment likely has weak potential.

Yield spread: The difference between a REIT's dividend yield and a benchmark, such as a ten-year government bond yield.

Author Biography

Mark Gordon is the managing editor of the *Gulf Coast Business Review*. The *Review* is an independently owned weekly publication covering business trends, companies, executives, and entrepreneurs on the Gulf Coast of Florida, from Tampa to Naples. Before the *Review*, Mark worked as a reporter for seven years at daily newspapers in Auburn, New York; West Chester, Pennsylvania; and Jacksonville, Florida. Mark lives in Lakewood Ranch, Florida, with his wife Elyse. This is his first book.

Sources

Block, R. (2006) *Investing in REITs*. New York, New York: Bloomberg Press.

Chan, S.H., Erickson, J., & Wang, K. (2003) *Real Estate Investment Trusts: Structure, Performance and Investment Opportunities*. New York, New York: Oxford University Press.

Garrigan, R. & Parsons, J., editors. (1998) *Real Estate Investment Trusts: Structure, Analysis, and Strategy*. New York, New York: McGraw-Hill.

Imperiale, R. (2006) *Getting Started in Real Estate Investment Trusts*. Hoboken, New Jersey: John Wiley & Sons, Inc.

Mullaney, J. (1998) REITs: *Building Profits with Real Estate Investment Trusts*. Hoboken, New Jersey: John Wiley & Sons, Inc.

Whiting, D. (2007) *Playing the REITs Game: Asia's New Real Estate Investment Trusts*. Asia: John Wiley & Sons, Inc.

Index